*Classic statements
of the American way*

THEY SPOKE
FOR
DEMOCRACY

Edited by FREDERICK C. PACKARD, JR.
Associate Professor of Public Speaking, Harvard University

CHARLES SCRIBNER'S SONS
NEW YORK

ACKNOWLEDGMENTS

The Portraits on the cover are used by permission of the following owners: PATRICK HENRY, the Colonial Williamsburg Collection; THOMAS JEFFERSON, the New York Historical Society; THEODORE ROOSEVELT, Brown Brothers; SAM HOUSTON, Library of Congress; ANDREW HAMILTON, the Historical Society of Pennsylvania; DANIEL WEBSTER, the Trustees of Dartmouth College; ALEXANDER HAMILTON, the National Gallery of Art, Washington, D.C.; DOUGLAS MACARTHUR, International News Photos; FRANKLIN D. ROOSEVELT, Wide World Photos; WOODROW WILSON, Princeton University; ABRAHAM LINCOLN, Library of Congress; GEORGE WASHINGTON, New York Public Library.

INTRODUCTION

Great Americans—men whose names are as familiar to you as your own—have given reasons for their faith in our Democracy, and have defined it or commented on it with varying degrees of eloquence and wisdom. Great emergencies called forth noble expressions of their social and political creed from men like Thomas Jefferson, Alexander Hamilton, Abraham Lincoln and both Theodore and Franklin Roosevelt. Many of the most notable of these statements have been gathered together in this book; the majority were made in public from a speaker's platform, but all are carefully wrought statements, rich in a lifetime's experience of thought, men and events. When some of them were first uttered, they met with fierce criticism; but they have withstood all attack and are today, by common consent, vital expressions of what Democracy in America has meant and means.

In selecting the materials for this book, the principal tests have been: "Did a particular speech or statement exert marked influence on public opinion and political action? Does it embody principles of abiding value in our national life? Has the judgment of time and the people testified to its truth?"

CONTENTS

*. . . all the high things that are said in
favour of rulers and of dignities, and upon
the side of power, will not be able to stop
people's mouths when they feel themselves
oppressed . . .*

From the
PLEA IN ZENGER'S TRIAL, 1735

*By Andrew Hamilton (Date of birth
unknown; deceased in 1741)*

ANDREW HAMILTON of Pennsylvania was a leader of the legal
profession during colonial times in America. His speech in defense of John Peter Zenger against a charge of criminal libel
was a high point in his distinguished career.

Zenger, publisher of the *New York Weekly Journal,* had
printed several biting comments in that newspaper on the public
conduct of Governor William Cosby, the blustering, arrogant
representative of the British Crown in New York Province. The
Governor had retaliated by arresting Zenger and by holding him
in jail for nearly ten months before trial. When the case was
heard at last, in April, 1735, Zenger's attorneys were disbarred
at the very outset for questioning the validity of appointment of
the judges.

Zenger's friends and other opponents of Governor Cosby
brought Andrew Hamilton up from Philadelphia to plead at a
rehearing of the case in August. Boldly and with great wit, he
challenged the perennial doctrine of the common law that a
jury had no right to inquire into the truth or falsity of an al-
leged libel. He overrode the protests of the prejudiced judges,

9

exasperated the Crown's attorney, and won a general verdict of "not guilty" for his client.

Gouverneur Morris called this trial and its outcome the "germ of American freedom." Our selection is reprinted with all its quaint spelling and punctuation from the verbatim account of the trial published in London in 1738.

. . . For tho' I own it to be base and unworthy to scandalize any Man, yet I think it is even vilanous to scandalize a Person of publick Character, and I will go so far into Mr. Attorney's Doctrine as to agree, that if the Faults, Mistakes, nay even the Vices of such a Person be private and personal, and don't affect the Peace of the Publick, or the Liberty or Property of our Neighbour, it is unmanly and unmannerly to expose them either by Word or Writing. But when a Ruler of a People brings his personal Failings, but much more his Vices, into his Administration, and the People find themselves affected by them, either in their Liberties or Properties, that will alter the Case mightily, and all the high Things that are said in Favour of Rulers, and of Dignities, and upon the side of Power, will not be able to stop People's Mouths when they feel themselves oppressed, I mean in a free Government. It is true in Times past it was a Crime to speak Truth, and in that terrible Court of Star-Chamber, many worthy and brave Men suffered for so doing; and yet even in that Court, and in those bad Times, a great and good Man durst say, what I hope will not be taken amiss of me to say in this Place, to wit, "The Practice of Informations for Libels is a Sword in the Hands of a wicked King, and an arrand Coward, to cut down and destroy the innocent; the one cannot, because of his high Station, and the other dares not, because of his Want of Courage, revenge himself in another Manner."

Mr. Attorney: Pray *Mr. Hamilton,* have a Care what you say, don't go too far neither, I don't like those Liberties.

Mr. Hamilton: Sure, Mr. Attorney, you won't make any Applications; all Men agree that we are governed by the best of Kings, and I cannot see the Meaning of Mr. Attorney's Caution: my well known Principles, and the Sense I have of the Blessings we enjoy under His present Majesty, makes it impossible for me to err, and I hope, even to be suspected, in that Point of Duty to my King. May it please Your Honour,

I was saying, That notwithstanding all the Duty and Reverence
claimed by Mr. Attorney to Men in Authority, they are not ex-
empt from observing the Rules of common Justice, either in
their private or publick Capacities; the Laws of our Mother
Country know no Exemption. It is true, Men in Power are
harder to be come at for Wrongs they do, either to a private
Person, or to the publick; especially a Governour in the Plantations, where they insist upon an Exemption from answering
Complaints of any Kind in their own Government. We are indeed told, and it is true they are obliged to answer a Suit in the
King's Courts at *Westminster,* for a Wrong done to any Person
here: But do we not know how impracticable this is to most
Men among us, to leave their Families (who depend upon their
Labour and Care for their Livelihood) and carry Evidences
to *Britain,* and at a great, nay, a far greater Expence than
almost any of us are able to bear, only to prosecute a Governour for an Injury done here. But when the Oppression
is general there is no Remedy even that Way, no, our Constitution has (blessed be God) given us an Opportunity, if
not to have such Wrongs redressed, yet by our Prudence and
Resolution we may in a great Measure prevent the committing
of such Wrongs, by making a Governour sensible that it is
his interest to be just to those under his Care; for such is the
Sense that Men in General (I mean Freemen) have of common Justice, that when they come to know, that a chief
Magistrate abuses the Power with which he is trusted, for
the good of the People, and is attempting to turn that very
Power against the Innocent, whether of high or low degree,
I say, Mankind in general seldom fail to interpose, and as
far as they can, prevent the Destruction of their fellow Subjects. And has it not often been seen (and I hope it will always
be seen) that when the Representatives of a free People are
by just Representations or Remonstrances, made sensible of
the Sufferings of their Fellow-Subjects, by the Abuse of Power
in the Hands of a Governour, they have declared (and loudly
too) that they were not obliged by any Law to support a
Governour who goes about to destroy a Province or Colony,

or their Priviledges, which by His Majesty he was appointed, and by the Law he is bound to protect and encourage. But I pray it may be considered of what Use is this mighty Priviledge, if every Man that suffers must be silent? And if a Man must be taken up as a Libeller, for telling his Sufferings to his Neighbour? I know it may be answered, *Have you not a Legislature? Have you not a House of Representatives to whom you may complain?* And to this I answer, we have. But what then? Is an Assembly to be troubled with every Injury done by a Governour? Or are they to hear of nothing but what those in the Administration will please to tell them? Or what Sort of a Tryal must a Man have? And how is he to be remedied; especially if the Case were, as I have known it to happen in *America* in my Time; That a Governour who has Places (I will not say Pensions, for I believe they seldom give that to another which they can take to themselves) to bestow, and can or will keep the same Assembly (after he has model'd them so as to get a Majority of the House in his Interest) for near *twice Seven Years* together? I pray, what Redress is to be expected for an honest Man, who makes his Complaint against a Governour, to an Assembly who may properly enough be said, to be made by the same Governour against whom the Complaint is made? The Thing answers itself. No, it is natural, it is a Priviledge, I will go farther, it is a Right which all Freemen claim, and are entitled to complain when they are hurt; they have a Right publickly to remonstrate the Abuses of Power, in the strongest Terms, to put their Neighbours upon their Guard, against the Craft of open Violence of Men in Authority, and to assert with Courage the Sense they have of the Blessings of Liberty, the Value they put upon it, and their Resolution at all Hazards to preserve it, as one of the greatest Blessings Heaven can bestow. And when a House of Assembly composed of honest Freemen sees the general Bent of the People's Inclinations, That is it which must and will (I'm sure it ought to) weigh with a Legislature, in Spite of all the Craft, Carressing and Cajoling, made use of by a Governour, to divert them from hearkning

to the Voice of their Country. As we all very well understand
the true Reason, why Gentlemen take so much Pains and
make such great Interest to be appointed Governours, so is
the Design of their Apointment not less manifest. We know
his Majesty's gracious Intentions to his Subjects; he desires
no more than that his People in the Plantations should be
kept up to their Duty and Allegiance to the Crown of *Great
Britain,* that Peace may be preserved amongst them, and
Justice impartially administered; that we may be governed
so as to render us useful to our Mother Country, by encouraging us to make and raise such Commodities as may be useful to *Great Britain.* But will any one say, that all or any of
these good Ends are to be effected, by a Governour's setting
his People together by the Ears, and by the Assistance of one
Part of the People to plague and plunder the other? The
Commission which Governours bear, while they execute the
Powers given them, according to the Intent of the Royal
Grantor, expressed in their Commissions, requires and deserves very great Reverence and Submission; but when a Governour departs from the Duty enjoyned him by his Sovereign,
and acts as if he was less accountable than the Royal Hand
that gave him all that Power and Honour which he is possessed of; this sets People upon examining and enquiring into
the Power, Authority and Duty of such a Magistrate, and
to compare those with his Conduct, and just as far as they find
he exceeds the Bounds of his Authority, or falls short in doing
impartial Justice to the People under his Administration, so
far they very often, in return, come short in their Duty to such
a Governour. For Power alone will not make a Man beloved,
and I have heard it observed, That the Man who was neither
good nor wise before his being made a Governour, never
mended upon his Preferment, but has been generally observed to be worse: For Men who are not endued with Wisdom and Virtue, can only be kept in Bounds by the Law;
and by how much the further they think themselves out of
the Reach of the Law, by so much the more wicked and
cruel Men are. I wish there were no Instances of the Kind at

this Day. And wherever this happens to be the Case of a Governour, unhappy are the People under his Administration, and in the End he will find himself so too; for the People will neither love him nor support him. I make no Doubt but there are those here, who are zealously concerned for the Success of this Prosecution, and yet I hope they are not many, and even some of those, I am perswaded (when they consider what Lengths such Prosecutions may be carried, and how deeply the Liberties of the People may be affected by such Means) will not all abide by their present Sentiments; I say, *Not All:* For the Man who from an Intimacy and Acquaintance with a Governour has conceived a personal Regard for him, the Man who has felt none of the Strokes of his Power, the Man who believes that a Governour has a Regard for him and confides in him, it is natural for such Men to wish well to the Affairs of such a Governour; and as they may be Men of Honour and Generosity, may, and no Doubt will, wish him Success, so far as the Rights and Priviledges of their Fellow Citizens are not affected. But as Men of Honour, I can apprehend nothing from them; they will never exceed that Point. There are others that are under stronger Obligations, and those are such, as are in some Sort engaged in Support of a Governour's Cause, by their own or their Relations Dependance on his Favour, for some Post or Preferment; such Men have what is commonly called Duty and Gratitude, to influence their Inclinations, and oblige them to go his Lengths. I know Men's Interests are very near to them, and they will do much, rather than forgoe the Favour of a Governour, and a Livelihood at the same Time; but I can with very just Grounds hope, even from those Men, whom I will suppose to be Men of Honour and Conscience too, that when they see, the Liberty of their Country is in Danger, either by their Concurrence, or even by their Silence, they will, like *Englishmen,* and like themselves, freely make a Sacrifice of any Preferment or Favour rather than be accessary to destroying the Liberties of their Country, and entailing Slavery upon their Posterity. There are indeed another set of Men, of whom I have no Hopes, I mean such, who lay aside all other Considerations, and are ready to joyn with Power in any Shapes, and with any Man or Sort of Men, by whose Means or Interest they may be assisted to gratify their Malice and Envy against those whom they have been pleased to hate; and that for no other Reason, but because they are Men of Abilities and Integrity, or at least are possessed of some valuable Qualities far superiour to their own. But as Envy is the Sin of the Devil, and therefore very hard, if at all, to be repented of, I will believe there are but few of this detestable and worthless Sort of Men, nor will their Opinions or Inclinations have any Influence upon this Tryal. But to proceed; I beg Leave to insist, That the Right of complaining or remonstrating is natural; and the Restraint upon this natural Right is the Law only, and that those Restraints can only extend to what is *false:* For as it is Truth alone which can excuse or justify any Man for complaining of a bad Administration, I as frankly agree, that nothing ought to excuse a Man who raises a false Charge or Accusation, even against a private Person, and that no manner of Allowance ought to be made to him, who does so against a publick Magistrate. *Truth* ought to govern the whole Affair of Libels, and yet the Party accused runs Risque enough even then: for if he fails of proving every Tittle of what he has wrote, and to the Satisfaction of the Court and Jury too, he may find to his Cost, that when the Prosecution is set on Foot by Men in Power, it seldom wants Friends to favour it. And from thence (it is said) has arisen the great Diversity of Opinions among Judges, about what Words were or were not scandalous or libellous. I believe it will be granted, that there is not greater Uncertainty in any Part of the Law, than about Words of Scandal; it would be mispending of the Court's Time to mention the Cases; they may be said to be numberless; and therefore the utmost Care ought to be taken in following Precedents; and the Times when the Judgments were given, which are quoted for Authorities in the Case of Libels, are much to be regarded. I think it will be agreed, That ever since the Time of the Star Chamber, where the most arbitrary and destructive Judgments and Opinions were given, that ever an *Englishman* heard of, at least in his own Country: I say, Prosecutions for Libels since the Time of that arbitrary Court, and until the glorious Revolution, have generally been set on Foot at the Instance of the Crown or its Ministers; and it is no small Reproach to the Law, that these Prosecutions were too often and too much countenanced by the Judges, who held their Places at Pleasure, (a disagreeable Tenure to any Officer, but a dangerous one in the Case of a Judge.) To say more to this Point may not be proper. And yet I cannot think it unwarrantable, to shew the unhappy Influence that a Sovereign has sometimes had, not only upon Judges, but even upon Parliaments themselves. . . .

This is the second Information for Libelling of a Governour that I have known in *America*. And the first, tho' it may look like a Romance, yet as it is true, I will beg Leave to mention it. Governour Nicholson, who happened to be offended with one of his Clergy, met him one Day upon the Road, and as was usual with him (under the Protection of his Commission) used the poor Parson with the worst of Language, threatened to cut off his Ears, slit his Nose, and at last to shoot him through the Head. The Parson being a reverend Man, continued all this Time uncovered in the Heat of the Sun, until he found an Opportunity to fly for it; and coming to a Neighbour's House felt himself very ill of a Fever, and immediately writes for a Doctor; and that his Physician might the better judge of his Distemper, he acquainted him with the Usage he had received; concluding, that the Governour was certainly mad, for that no Man in his Senses would have behaved in that manner. The Doctor unhappily shews the Parsons letter; the Governour came to hear of it; and so an Information was prefered against the poor Man for saying *he believed the Governour was mad;* and it was laid in the Information to be *false, scandalous and wicked, and wrote with Intent to move Sedition among the People, and bring His Excellency into Contempt.* But by an

Order from the late Queen *Anne,* there was a Stop put to
that Prosecution, with sundry others set on foot by the same
Governour, against Gentlemen of the greatest Worth and
Honour in that Government.

And may not I be allowed, after all this, to say, That by a
little Countenance, almost any Thing which a Man writes,
may, with the Help of that useful Term of Art, called an
Innuendo, be construed to be a Libel, according to Mr. Attorney's Definition of it, That *whether the Words are Spoke
of a Person of a publick Character, or of a private Man,
whether dead or living, good or bad, true or false,* all make
a Libel; for according to Mr. Attorney, *after a Man hears a
Writing read, or reads and repeats it, or laughs at it, they are
all punishable.* It is true, Mr. Attorney is so good as to allow,
after the Party knows it to be a Libel, but he is not so kind
as to take the Man's Word for it.

(Here were several Cases put to shew, That tho' what a
Man writes of a Governour was true, proper and necessary,
yet according to the forgoing Doctrine it might be construed to be a Libel: But Mr. *Hamilton* after the Tryal
was over, being informed, That some of the Cases he had
put had really happened in this Government, he declared
he had never heard of any such; and as he meant no personal Reflections, he was sorry he had mentioned them, and
therefore they are omitted here.)

Mr. Hamilton: If a Libel is understood in the large and
unlimited Sense urged by Mr. Attorney, there is scarce a
Writing I know that may not be called a Libel, or scarce
any Person safe from being called to Account as a Libeller:
For *Moses,* meek as he was, libelled *Cain;* and who is it that
has not libelled the Devil? For according to Mr. Attorney, it
is no Justification to say one has a bad Name. *Echard* has
libelled our good King *William: Burnet* has libelled among
many others King *Charles* and King *James;* and *Rapin* has
libelled them all. How must a Man speak or write, or what
must he hear, read, or sing? Or when must he laugh, so as to

be secure from being taken up as a Libeller? I sincerely believe, that were some Persons to go thro' the Streets of *New-York* now-a-days, and read a Part of the Bible, if it was not known to be such, Mr. Attorney, with the Help of his Innuendos, would easily turn it into a Libel. As for Instance, *Is.* ix. 16. *The Leaders of the People cause them to err, and they that are led by them are destroyed.* But should Mr. Attorney go about to make this a Libel, he would read it thus; *The Leaders of the People* (innuendo, the Governour and Council of *New-York*) *cause them* (innuendo, the People of this Province) *to err, and they* (the Governour and Council meaning) *are destroyed* (innuendo, are deceived into the Loss of their Liberty) which is the worst Kind of Destruction. Or if some Persons should publickly repeat, in a Manner not pleasing to his Betters, the 10*th* and 11*th* Verses of the lvi*th*. Chap. of the same Book, there Mr. Attorney would have a large Field to display his Skill, in the artful Application of his Innuendos. The Words are, *His Watchmen are all blind, they are ignorant, Yea, they are greedy Dogs, that can never have enough.* But to make them a Libel, there is according to Mr. Attorney's Doctrine, no more wanting but the Aid of his Skill, in the right adapting his *Innuendos.* As for Instance; *His Watchmen* (innuendo, the Governour's Council and Assembly) *are blind, they are ignorant* (innuendo, will not see the dangerous Designs of His Excellency) *Yea, they* (the Governour and Council meaning) *are greedy Dogs, which can never have enough* (innuendo, enough of Riches and Power.) Such an Instance as this is seems only fit be to laugh'd at; but I may appeal to Mr. Attorney himself, whether these are not at least equally proper to be applied to His Excellency and His Ministers, as some of the Inferences and *Innuendos* in his Information against my Client. Then if Mr. Attorney is at Liberty to come into Court, and file an Information in the King's Name, without Leave, who is secure, whom he is pleased to prosecute as a Libeller? And as the Crown Law is contended for in bad Times, there is no Remedy for the greatest Oppression of this Sort, even tho' the Party prosecuted is acquitted with Honour. And give me Leave to say, as great Men as any in *Britain,* have boldly asserted, That the Mode of prosecuting by Information (when a Grand Jury will not find *billa vera*) is a national Grievance, and greatly inconsistent with that Freedom, which the Subjects of *England* enjoy in most other Cases. But if we are so unhappy as not to be able to ward off this Stroke of Power directly, yet let us take Care not to be cheated out of our Liberties, by Forms and Appearances; let us always be sure that the Charge in the Information is made out clearly even beyond a Doubt; for tho' Matters in the Information may be called *Form* upon Tryal, yet they may be, and often have been found to be *Matters of Substance* upon giving Judgment.

Gentlemen, the danger is great, in proportion to the Mischief that may happen, through our too great Credulity. A proper Confidence in a Court is commendable; but as the Verdict (whatever it is) will be yours, you ought to refer no Part of your Duty to the Discretion of other Persons. If you should be of Opinion, that there is no Falsehood in Mr. *Zenger's* Papers, you will, nay (pardon me for the Expression) you ought to say so; because you don't know whether, others (I mean the Court) may be of that Opinion. It is your Right to do so, and there is much depending upon your Resolution, as well as upon your Integrity. . . .

I hope to be pardon'd, Sir, for my Zeal upon this Occasion; It is an old and wise Caution, *That when our Neighbour's House is on Fire, we ought to take Care of our own.* For tho', blessed be God, I live in a Government where Liberty is well understood, and freely enjoy'd; yet Experience has shewn us all (I'm sure it has to me) that a bad Precedent in one Government, is soon set up for an Authority in another; and therefore I cannot but think it mine, and every Honest Man's Duty, that (while we pay all due Obedience to Men in Authority) we ought at the same Time to be upon our Guard against Power, wherever we apprehend that it may affect Ourselves or our Fellow-Subjects.

I am truly very unequal to such an Undertaking on many

Accounts. And you see I labour under the Weight of many Years, and am born down with great Infirmities of Body; yet Old and Weak as I am, I should think it my Duty, if required, to go the utmost Part of the Land, where my Service cou'd be of any Use in assisting to quench the Flame of Prosecutions upon Informations, set on Foot by the Government, to deprive a People of the Right of Remonstrating, (and complaining too) of the arbitrary Attempts of Men in Power. Men who injure and appress the People under their Administration provoke them to cry out and complain; and then make that very Complaint the Foundation for new Oppressions and Prosecutions. I wish I could say there were no instances of this kind.

But to conclude; the Question before the Court and you, Gentlemen of the Jury, is not of small nor private Concern, it is not the Cause of a poor Printer, nor of *New-York* alone, which you are now trying: No! It may in its Consequence, affect every Freeman that lives under a British Government on the Main of *America*. It is the best Cause. It is the Cause of Liberty; and I make no Doubt but your upright Conduct, this Day, will not only entitle you to the Love and Esteem of your Fellow-Citizens; but every Man, who prefers Freedom to a Life of Slavery, will bless and honour You, as Men who have baffled the Attempt of Tyranny; and by an impartial and uncorrupt Verdict, have laid a noble Foundation for securing to ourselves, our Posterity, and our Neighbours, That, to which Nature and Laws of our Country have given us a Right,—The Liberty—both of exposing and opposing arbitrary Power (in these Parts of the World, at least) by speaking and writing Truth. . . .

Shall we acquire the means of effectual re-
sistance by lying supinely on our backs—?

AMERICAN LIBERTY

By Patrick Henry (1736–1799)

THIS FAMOUS ADDRESS was given before the second Virginia Convention of Delegates on March 23, 1775. The proceedings of the
First Continental Congress (in which Patrick Henry had taken
an active part) having been approved, a bitter debate ensued on
resolutions which Henry offered for putting the colony into an
immediate "posture of defense" by raising and training a militia.
This speech, with its resounding final sentence, was made in the
course of the debate, but no contemporary written record of it
survives. The version we have was given by William Wirt in his
Life and Character of Patrick Henry, written in 1817; it is based
on tradition and old men's recollections of what Henry said, yet
its fidelity to the mood of the time, its embodiment of the spirit
behind our rejection of British authority, remain unchallenged.

MR. PRESIDENT: No man thinks more highly than I do of the patriotism, as well as abilities, of the very worthy gentlemen who have just addressed the House. But different men often see the same subject in different lights; and, therefore, I hope that it will not be thought disrespectful to those gentlemen, if, entertaining as I do, opinions of a character very opposite to theirs, I shall speak forth my sentiments freely and without reserve. This is no time for ceremony. The question before the House is one of awful moment to this country. For my own part I consider it as nothing less than a question of freedom or slavery; and in proportion to the magnitude of the subject ought to be the freedom of the debate. It is only in this way that we can hope to arrive at truth, and fulfil the great responsibility which we hold to God and our country. Should I keep back my opinions at such a time, through fear of giving offence, I should consider myself as guilty of treason towards my country, and of an act of disloyalty towards the majesty of heaven, which I revere above all earthly kings.

Mr. President, it is natural to man to indulge in the illusions of hope. We are apt to shut our eyes against a painful truth, and listen to the song of that siren, till she transforms us into beasts. Is this the part of wise men, engaged in a great and arduous struggle for liberty? Are we disposed to be of the number of those who, having eyes, see not, and having ears, hear not, the things which so nearly concern their temporal salvation? For my part, whatever anguish of spirit it may cost, I am willing to know the whole truth; to know the worst and to provide for it.

I have but one lamp by which my feet are guided; and that is the lamp of experience. I know of no way of judging of the future but by the past. And judging by the past, I wish to know what there has been in the conduct of the British ministry for the last ten years, to justify those hopes with which gentlemen have been pleased to solace themselves and the House? Is it that insidious smile with which our petition has been lately received? Trust it not, sir; it will prove a snare to your feet. Suffer not yourselves to be betrayed with a kiss. Ask yourselves how this gracious reception of our petition comports with these war-like preparations which cover our waters and darken our land. Are fleets and armies necessary to a work of love and reconciliation? Have we shown ourselves so unwilling to be reconciled, that force must be called in to win back our love? Let us not deceive ourselves, sir. These are the implements of war and subjugation; the last arguments to which kings resort. I ask gentlemen, sir, what means this martial array, if its purpose be not to force us to submission? Can gentlemen assign any other possible motives for it? Has Great Britain any enemy, in this quarter of the world, to call for all this accumulation of navies and armies? No, sir, she has none. They are meant for us; they can be meant for no other. They are sent over to bind and rivet upon us those chains which the British ministry have been so long forging. And what have we to oppose to them? Shall we try argument? Sir, we have been trying that for the last ten years. Have we anything new to offer on the subject? Nothing. We have held the subject up in every light of which it is capable; but it has been all in vain. Shall we resort to entreaty and humble supplication? What terms shall we find which have not been already exhausted? Let us not, I beseech you, sir, deceive ourselves longer. Sir, we have done everything that could be done, to avert the storm which is now coming on. We have petitioned; we have remonstrated; we have supplicated; we have prostrated ourselves before the throne, and have implored its interposition to arrest the tyrannical hands of the ministry and Parliament. Our petitions have been slighted; our remonstrances have produced additional violence and insult; our supplications have been disregarded; and we have been spurned, with contempt, from the foot of the throne. In vain, after these things, may we indulge the fond hope of peace and reconciliation. There is no longer any room for hope. If we wish to be free—if we mean to preserve inviolate those inestimable privileges for which we have been so long contending—if we mean not basely to abandon the noble struggle in which we have been so long engaged, and which we have pledged ourselves never to abandon until the glorious object of our contest shall be obtained, we must fight! I repeat it, sir, we must fight! An appeal to arms and to the God of Hosts is all that is left us!

They tell us, sir, that we are weak; unable to cope with so formidable an adversary. But when shall we be stronger? Will it be the next week, or the next year? Will it be when we are totally disarmed, and when a British guard shall be stationed in every house? Shall we gather strength by irresolution and inaction? Shall we acquire the means of effectual resistance, by lying supinely on our backs, and hugging the delusive phantom of hope, until our enemies shall have bound us hand and foot? Sir, we are not weak, if we make a proper use of the means which the God of nature hath placed in our power. Three millions of people, armed in the holy cause of liberty, and in such a country as that which we possess, are invincible by any force which our enemy can send against us. Besides, sir, we shall not fight our battles alone. There is a just God who presides over the destinies of nations; and who will raise up friends to fight our battles for us. The battle, sir, is not to the strong alone; it is to the vigilant, the active, the brave. Besides, sir, we have no election. If we were base enough to desire it, it is now too late to retire from the contest. There is no retreat, but in submission and slavery! Our chains are forged! Their clanking may be heard on the plains of Boston! The war is inevitable—and let it come! I repeat it, sir, let it come!

It is in vain, sir, to extenuate the matter. Gentlemen may cry peace, peace—but there is no peace. The war is actually begun! The next gale that sweeps from the north will bring to our ears the clash of resounding arms! Our brethren are already in the field! Why stand we here idle? What is it that gentlemen wish? What would they have? Is life so dear, or peace so sweet, as to be purchased at the price of chains and slavery? Forbid it, Almighty God! I know not what course others may take; but as for me, give me liberty, or give me death!

It is our duty to draw from nature, from reason, from examples, the best principles of policy, and to pursue and apply them in the formation of our government.

THE FEDERAL CONSTITUTION

By Alexander Hamilton (1757–1804)

ALEXANDER HAMILTON had served as a delegate from New York to the Constitutional Convention in Philadelphia. When the Constitution was in its final form he signed it for New York, and then hastened home to secure its ratification by his native State. The *Federalist* papers, which he, John Jay and James Madison contributed to the press, were effective in winning popular support for the new Constitution, but the part he played at the New York ratifying convention was equally important. The convention, held at Poughkeepsie, N. Y., during June and July, 1788, was filled with men antagonistic to the Constitution, and only the closest and most sustained argument on the part of its friends won final ratification by a majority of three votes. The present speech was delivered on June 24, 1788, and was in reply to a proposed amendment that no person should be eligible as a Senator for more than six years in any term of twelve years, and that the State legislatures should have the power to recall their Senators and elect substitutes.

I AM PERSUADED, Mr. Chairman, that I in my turn shall be indulged in addressing the committee. We all, in equal sincerity, profess to be anxious for the establishment of a republican government, on a safe and solid basis. It is the object of the wishes of every honest man in the United States, and I presume I shall not be disbelieved, when I declare, that it is an object of all others, the nearest and most dear to my own heart. The means of accomplishing this great purpose, become the most important study which can interest mankind. It is our duty to examine all those means with peculiar attention, and to choose the best and most effectual. It is our duty to draw from nature, from reason, from examples, the best principles of policy, and to pursue and apply them in the formation of our government. We should contemplate and compare the systems which, in this examination, come under our view; distinguish, with a careful eye, the defects and excellencies of each, and discarding the former, incorporate the latter, as far as circumstances will admit, into our constitution. If we pursue a different course and neglect this duty, we shall probably disappoint the expectations of our country and of the world.

In the commencement of a revolution, which received its birth from the usurpations of tyranny, nothing was more natural than that the public mind should be influenced by an extreme spirit of jealousy. To resist these encroachments, and to nourish this spirit, was the great object of all our public and private institutions. The zeal for liberty became predominant and excessive. In forming our confederation, this passion alone seemed to actuate us, and we appear to have had no other view than to secure ourselves from despotism. The object certainly was a valuable one, and deserved our utmost attention. But, sir, there is another object, equally important, and which our enthusiasm rendered us little capable of regarding: I mean a principle of strength and stability in the organization of our government, and vigor in its operations. This purpose can never be accomplished but by the establishment of some select body, formed peculiarly upon this principle. There are few positions more demonstrable than that there should be in every republic, some permanent body to correct the prejudices, check the intemperate passions, and regulate the fluctuations of a popular assembly. It is evident, that a body instituted for these purposes, must be so formed as to exclude, as much as possible, from its own character, those infirmities, and that mutability which it is designed to remedy. It is therefore necessary that it should be small, that it should hold its authority during a considerable period, and that it should have such an independence in the exercise of its powers as will divest it as much as possible of local prejudices. It should be so formed as to be the centre of political knowledge, to pursue always a steady line of conduct, and to reduce every irregular propensity to system. Without this establishment, we may make experiments without end, but shall never have an efficient government.

It is an unquestionable truth, that the body of the people in every country desire sincerely its prosperity; but it is equally unquestionable, that they do not possess the discernment and stability necessary for systematic government. To deny that they are frequently led into the grossest errors by misinformation and passion, would be a flattery which their own good-sense must despise. That branch of administration especially, which involves our political relations with foreign states, a community will ever be incompetent to. These truths are not often held up in public assemblies; but they cannot be unknown to any who hear me. From these principles it follows, that there ought to be two distinct bodies in our government; one, which shall be immediately constituted by and peculiarly represent the people, and possess all the popular features; another, formed upon the principle, and for the purposes before explained. Such considerations as these induced the convention who formed your State constitution, to institute a senate upon the present plan. The history of an-

cient and modern republics had taught them, that many of
the evils which these republics suffered, arose from the want
of a certain balance and mutual control indispensable to a
wise administration; they were convinced that popular assemblies are frequently misguided by ignorance, by sudden
impulses, and the intrigues of ambitious men; and that some
firm barrier against these operations was necessary; they therefore instituted your Senate, and the benefits we have experienced have fully justified their conceptions.

Now, sir, what is the tendency of the proposed amendment?
To take away the stability of government, by depriving the
Senate of its permanency; to make this body subject to the
same weakness and prejudices which are incident to popular
assemblies, and which it was instituted to correct; and by thus
assimilating the complexion of the two branches, destroy the
balance between them. The amendment will render the Senator a slave to all the capricious humors among the people. It
will probably be here suggested, that the legislatures, not the
people, are to have the power of recall. Without attempting
to prove that the legislatures must be, in a great degree, the
image of the multitude, in respect to federal affairs, and that
the same prejudices and factions will prevail; I insist, that
in whatever body the power of recall is vested, the Senator
will perpetually feel himself in such a state of vassalage and
dependence, that he never can possess that firmness which is
necessary to the discharge of his great duty to the Union.

Gentlemen, in their reasoning, have placed the interests of
the several States and those of the United States in contrast;
this is not a fair view of the subject; they must necessarily be
involved in each other. What we apprehend is, that some sinister prejudice, or some prevailing passion, may assume the
form of a genuine interest. The influence of these is as powerful as the most permanent conviction of the public good;
and against this influence we ought to provide. The local interests of a State ought in every case to give way to the interests of the Union; for when a sacrifice of one or the other is
necessary, the former becomes only an apparent, partial in-

terest, and should yield, on the principle that the small good ought never to oppose the great one. When you assemble from your several counties in the legislature, were every member to be guided only by the apparent interest of his county, government would be impracticable. There must be a perpetual accommodation and sacrifice of local advantage to general expediency; but the spirit of a mere popular assembly would rarely be actuated by this important principle. It is therefore absolutely necessary that the Senate should be so formed, as to be unbiassed by false conceptions of the real interests, or undue attachment to the apparent good of their several States.

Gentlemen indulge too many unreasonable apprehensions of danger to the State governments; they seem to suppose that the moment you put men into a national council, they become corrupt and tyrannical, and lose all their affection for their fellow-citizens. But can we imagine that the Senators will ever be so insensible of their own advantage, as to sacrifice the genuine interest of their constituents? The State governments are essentially necessary to the form and spirit of the general system. As long, therefore, as Congress have a full conviction of this necessity, they must, even upon principles purely national, have as firm an attachment to the one as to the other. This conviction can never leave them, unless they become madmen. While the constitution continues to be read, and its principles known, the States must, by every rational man, be considered as essential, component parts of the Union; and therefore the idea of sacrificing the former to the latter is wholly inadmissible.

The objectors do not advert to the natural strength and resources of State governments, which will ever give them an important superiority over the general government. If we compare the nature of their different powers, or the means of popular influence which each possesses, we shall find the advantage entirely on the side of the States. This consideration, important as it is, seems to have been little attended to. The aggregate number of representatives throughout the States

may be two thousand. Their personal influence will, therefore, be proportionally more extensive than that of one or two
hundred men in Congress. The State establishments of civil
and military officers of every description, infinitely surpassing
in number any possible correspondent establishments in the
general government, will create such an extent and complica-
tion of attachments, as will ever secure the predilection and
support of the people. Whenever, therefore, Congress shall
meditate any infringement of the State constitutions, the
great body of the people will naturally take part with their
domestic representatives. Can the general government withstand such a united opposition? Will the people suffer themselves to be stripped of their privileges? Will they suffer their
legislatures to be reduced to a shadow and a name? The idea
is shocking to common-sense.

From the circumstances already explained, and many others
which might be mentioned, results a complicated, irresistible
check, which must ever support the existence and importance
of the State governments. The danger, if any exists, flows from
an opposite source. The probable evil is, that the general
government will be too dependent on the State legislatures,
too much governed by their prejudices, and too obsequious to
their humors; that the States, with every power in their hands,
will make encroachments on the national authority, till the
Union is weakened and dissolved.

Every member must have been struck with an observation
of a gentleman from Albany. Do what you will, says he, local
prejudices and opinions will go into the Government. What!
shall we then form a constitution to cherish and strengthen
these prejudices? Shall we confirm the distemper instead of
remedying it? It is undeniable that there must be a control
somewhere. Either the general interest is to control the particular interests, or the contrary. If the former, then certainly
the Government ought to be so framed, as to render the power
of control efficient to all intents and purposes; if the latter,
a striking absurdity follows; the controlling powers must be
as numerous as the varying interests, and the operations of

government must therefore cease; or the moment you accommodate these different interests, which is the only way to set the Government in motion, you establish a general controlling power. Thus, whatever constitutional provisions are made to the contrary, every government will be at last driven to the necessity of subjecting the partial to the universal interest. The gentlemen ought always, in their reasoning, to distinguish between the real, genuine good of a state, and the opinions and prejudices which may prevail respecting it; the latter may be opposed to the general good, and consequently ought to be sacrificed; the former is so involved in it, that it never can be sacrificed. Sir, the main design of the convention, in forming the Senate, was to prevent fluctuations and cabals. With this view, they made that body small and to exist for a considerable period. Have they executed this design too far? The senators are to serve six years. This is only two years longer than the senators of this State hold their places. One-third of the members are to go out every two years; and in six, the whole body may be changed. Prior to the revolution, the representatives in the several colonies were elected for different periods; for three years, for seven years, etc. Were those bodies ever considered as incapable of representing the people, or as too independent of them? There is one circumstance which will have a tendency to increase the dependence of the senators on the States, in proportion to the duration of their appointments. As the State legislatures are in continual fluctuation, the senator will have more attachments to form, and consequently a greater difficulty of maintaining his place, than one of shorter duration. He will therefore be more cautious and industrious to suit his conduct to the wishes of his constituents.

Sir, when you take a view of all the circumstances which have been recited, you will certainly see that the senators will constantly look up to the state governments with an eye of dependence and affection. If they are ambitious to continue in office, they will make every prudent arrangement for this purpose, and whatever may be their private sentiments of politics, they will be convinced that the surest means of obtaining a re-election will be a uniform attachment to the interests of their several States.

The gentlemen, to support their amendment, have observed that the power of recall, under the old government, has never been exercised. There is no reasoning from this. The experience of a few years, under peculiar circumstances, can afford no probable security that it never will be carried into execution with unhappy effects. A seat in Congress has been less an object of ambition, and the arts of intrigue, consequently, have been less practised. Indeed, it has been difficult to find men who were willing to suffer the mortifications to which so feeble a government and so dependent a station exposed them.

Sir, if you consider but a moment the purposes for which the Senate was instituted, and the nature of the business which they are to transact, you will see the necessity of giving them duration. They, together with the President, are to manage all our concerns with foreign nations; they must understand all their interests and their political systems. This knowledge is not soon acquired—but a very small part is gained in the closet. Is it desirable, then, that new and unqualified members should be continually thrown into that body? When public bodies are engaged in the exercise of general powers, you cannot judge of the propriety of their conduct but from the result of their systems. They may be forming plans which require time and diligence to bring to maturity. It is necessary, therefore, that they should have a considerable and fixed duration, that they may make their calculations accordingly. If they are to be perpetually fluctuating they can never have that responsibility which is so important in republican governments. In bodies subject to frequent changes, great political plans must be conducted by members in succession; a single assembly can have but a partial agency in them, and consequently cannot properly be answerable for the final event. Considering the Senate, therefore, with a view to responsibility, duration is a very interesting and essential quality. There is another view in which duration in the Senate appears necessary. A government, changeable in its policy, must soon lose its sense of national character, and forfeit the respect of foreigners. Senators will not be solicitous for the reputation of public measures in which they have had but a temporary concern, and will feel lightly the burden of public disapprobation in proportion to the number of those who partake of the censure. Our political rivals will ever consider our mutable counsels as evidence of deficient wisdom, and will be little apprehensive of our arriving at any exalted station in the scale of power. Such are the internal and external disadvantages which would result from the principle contended for. Were it admitted, I am fully persuaded, sir, that prejudices would govern the public deliberations, and passions rage in the councils of the Union. If it were necessary, I could illustrate my subject by historical facts; I could travel through an extensive field of detail, and demonstrate that wherever the fatal principle of—the head suffering the control of the members, has operated, it has proved a fruitful source of commotions and disorder.

This, sir, is the first fair opportunity that has been offered of deliberately correcting the errors in government. Instability has been a prominent and very defective feature in most republican systems. It is the first to be seen and the last to be lamented by a philosophical inquirer. It has operated most banefully in our infant republics. It is necessary that we apply an immediate remedy, and eradicate the poisonous principle from our government. If this be not done, sir, we shall feel, and posterity will be convulsed by a painful malady.

*There can be no greater error than to ex-
pect or calculate upon real favors from
nation to nation.*

A FAREWELL ADDRESS
TO THE AMERICAN PEOPLE

By George Washington (1732–1799)

THE IMMEDIATE occasion for this address was Washington's desire to disclaim any wish for a third Presidential term. He had
already expressed many of the thoughts herein contained in a
letter written in 1792. However, as well as achieving its specific
purpose, the address as we have it constitutes a political testament
—a body of advice which has had very great influence on our
history and political thinking. Extreme admirers of Alexander
Hamilton claim that he deserves a major share of the credit for
this address, first published on September 17, 1796; it is more
correct to say that Hamilton aided in the composition, but that
the ideas were Washington's own. The present text is a slightly
shortened version of the original.

FRIENDS AND FELLOW CITIZENS: The period for a new election of a citizen to administer the Executive Government of the United States being not far distant, and the time actually arrived when your thoughts must be employed in designating the person who is to be clothed with that important trust, it appears to me proper, especially as it may conduce to more distinct expression of the public voice, that I should now apprise you of the resolution I have formed to decline being considered among the number of those out of whom a choice is to be made. . . .

The impressions with which I first undertook the arduous trust were explained on the proper occasion. In the discharge of this trust I will only say that I have, with good intentions, contributed toward the organization and administration of the Government the best exertions of which a very fallible judgment was capable. Not unconscious in the outset of the inferiority of my qualifications, experience in my own eyes, perhaps still more in the eyes of others, has strengthened the motives to diffidence of myself; and every day the increasing weight of years admonishes me more and more that the shade of retirement is as necessary to me as it will be welcome. Satisfied that if any circumstances have given peculiar value to my services they were temporary, I have the consolation to believe that, while choice and prudence invite me to quit the political scene, patriotism does not forbid it. . . .

Here, perhaps, I ought to stop. But a solicitude for your welfare which can not end with my life, and the apprehension of danger natural to that solicitude, urge me on an occasion like the present to offer to your solemn contemplation and to recommend to our frequent review some sentiments which are the result of much reflection, of no inconsiderable observation, and which appear to me all important to the permanency of your felicity as a people. . . .

Interwoven as is the love of liberty with every ligament

of your hearts, no recommendation of mine is necessary to fortify or confirm the attachment.

The unity of government which constitutes you one people is also now dear to you. It is justly so, for it is a main pillar in the edifice of your real independence, the support of your tranquillity at home, your peace abroad, of your safety, of your prosperity, of that very liberty which you so highly prize. But as it is easy to foresee that from different causes and from different quarters much pains will be taken, many artifices employed, to weaken in your minds the conviction of this truth, as this is the point in your political fortress against which the batteries of internal and external enemies will be most constantly and actively (though often covertly and insidiously) directed, it is of infinite moment that you should properly estimate the immense value of your national union to your collective and individual happiness; that you should cherish a cordial, habitual, and immovable attachment to it; accustoming yourselves to think and speak of it as of the palladium of your political safety and prosperity; watching for its preservation with jealous anxiety; discountenancing whatever may suggest even a suspicion that it can in any event be abandoned, and indignantly frowning upon the first dawning of every attempt to alienate any portion of our country from the rest or to enfeeble the sacred ties which now link together the various parts.

For this you have every inducement of sympathy and interest. Citizens by birth or choice of a common country, that country has a right to concentrate your affections. The name of American, which belongs to you in your national capacity, must always exalt the just pride of patriotism more than any appellation derived from local discriminations. With slight shades of difference, you have the same religion, manners, habits, and political principles. You have in a common cause fought and triumphed together. The independence and liberty you possess are the work of joint councils and joint efforts, of common dangers, sufferings, and successes.

But these considerations, however powerfully they address

themselves to your sensibility, are greatly outweighed by those which apply more immediately to your interest. Here every portion of our country finds the most commanding motives for carefully guarding and preserving the union of the whole.

The *North,* in an unrestrained intercourse with the *South,* protected by the equal laws of a common government, finds in the productions of the latter great additional resources of maritime and commercial enterprise and precious materials of manufacturing industry. The *South,* in the same intercourse, benefiting by the same agency of the *North,* sees its agriculture grow and its commerce expand. Turning partly into its own channels the seamen of the *North,* it finds its particular navigation invigorated; and while it contributes in different ways to nourish and increase the general mass of the national navigation, it looks forward to the protection of a maritime strength to which itself is unequally adapted. The *East,* in a like intercourse with the *West,* already finds, and in the progressive improvement of interior communications by land and water will more and more find, a valuable vent for the commodities which it brings from abroad or manufactures at home. The *West* derives from the *East* supplies requisite to its growth and comfort, and what is perhaps of still greater consequence, it must of necessity owe the *secure* enjoyment of indispensable *outlets* for its own productions to the weight, influence, and the future maritime strength of the Atlantic side of the Union, directed by an indissoluble community of interest as *one nation.* Any other tenure by which the *West* can hold this essential advantage, whether derived from its own separate strength or from an apostate and unnatural connection with any foreign power, must be intrinsically precarious.

While, then, every part of our country thus feels an immediate and particular interest in union, all the parts combined can not fail to find in the united mass of means and efforts greater strength, greater resource, proportionably greater security from external danger, a less frequent interruption of their peace by foreign nations, and what is of inestimable value, they must derive from union an exemption from those broils and wars between themselves which so frequently afflict neighboring countries not tied together by the same governments, which their own rivalships alone would be sufficient to produce, but which opposite foreign alliances, attachments, and intrigues would stimulate and imbitter. Hence, likewise, they will avoid the necessity of those overgrown military establishments which, under any form of government, are inauspicious to liberty, and which are to be regarded as particularly hostile to republican liberty. In this sense it is that your union ought to be considered as a main prop of your liberty, and that the love of the one ought to endear to you the preservation of the other. . . .

Is there a doubt whether a common government can embrace so large a sphere? Let experience solve it. To listen to mere speculation in such a case were criminal. It is well worth a fair and full experiment. With such powerful and obvious motives to union affecting all parts of our country, while experience shall not have demonstrated its impracticability, there will always be reason to distrust the patriotism of those who in any quarter may endeavor to weaken its bands.

In contemplating the causes which may disturb our union it occurs as matter of serious concern that any ground should have been furnished for characterizing parties by *geographical* discriminations—*Northern* and *Southern, Atlantic* and *Western*—whence designing men may endeavor to excite a belief that there is a real difference of local interests and views. One of the expedients of party to acquire influence within particular districts is to misrepresent the opinions and aims of other districts. You can not shield yourselves too much against the jealousies and heartburnings which spring from these misrepresentations; they tend to render alien to each other those who ought to be bound together by fraternal affection. . . .

To the efficacy and permanency of your union a government for the whole is indispensable. No alliances, however strict, between the parts can be an adequate substitute. They must inevitably experience the infractions and interruptions which all alliances in all times have experienced. Sensible of this momentous truth, you have improved upon your first essay by the adoption of a Constitution of Government better calculated than your former for an intimate union and for the efficacious management of your common concerns. This Government, the offspring of our own choice, uninfluenced and unawed, adopted upon full investigation and mature deliberation, completely free in its principles, in the distribution of its powers, uniting security with energy, and containing within itself a provision for its own amendment, has a just claim to your confidence and your support. Respect for its authority, compliance with its laws, acquiescence in its measures, are duties enjoined by the fundamental maxims of true liberty. The basis of our political systems is the right of the people to make and to alter their constitutions of government. But the constitution which at any time exists till changed by an explicit and authentic act of the whole people is sacredly obligatory upon all. The very idea of the power and the right of the people to establish government presupposes the duty of every individual to obey the established government. . . .

Toward the preservation of your Government and the permanency of your present happy state, it is requisite not only that you steadily discountenance irregular oppositions to its acknowledged authority, but also that you resist with care the spirit of innovation upon its principles, however specious the pretexts. One method of assault may be to effect in the forms of the Constitution alterations which will impair the energy of the system, and thus to undermine what can not be directly overthrown. In all the changes to which you may be invited remember that time and habit are at least as necessary to fix the true character of governments as of other human institutions; that experience is the surest standard by which to test the real tendency of the existing constitution of a country; that facility in changes upon the credit of mere hypothesis and opinion exposes to perpetual change, from the endless variety of hypothesis and opinion; and remember especially that for the efficient management of your common interests in a country so extensive as ours a government of as much vigor as is consistent with the perfect security of liberty is indispensable. Liberty itself will find in such a government, with powers properly distributed and adjusted, its surest guardian. It is, indeed, little else than a name where the government is too feeble to withstand the enterprises of faction, to confine each member of the society within the limits prescribed by the laws, and to maintain all in the secure and tranquil enjoyment of the rights of person and property.

I have already intimated to you the danger of parties in the State, with particular reference to the founding of them on geographical discriminations. Let me now take a more comprehensive view, and warn you in the most solemn manner against the baneful effects of the spirit of party generally.

This spirit, unfortunately, is inseparable from our nature, having its root in the strongest passions of the human mind. It exists under different shapes in all governments, more or less stifled, controlled, or repressed; but in those of the popular form it is seen in its greatest rankness and is truly their worst enemy. . . .

It serves always to distract the public councils and enfeeble the public administration. It agitates the community with ill-founded jealousies and false alarms; kindles the animosity of one part against another; foments occasionally riot and insurrection. It opens the door to foreign influence and corruption, which find a facilitated access to the government itself through the channels of party passion. Thus the policy and the will of one country are subjected to the policy and will of another.

There is an opinion that parties in free countries are useful checks upon the administration of the government, and serve to keep alive the spirit of liberty. This within certain limits is probably true; and in governments of a monarchical cast patriotism may look with indulgence, if not with favor, upon the spirit of party. But in those of the popular character, in governments purely elective, it is a spirit not to be encouraged. From their natural tendency it is certain there will always be enough of that spirit for every salutary purpose; and there being constant danger of excess, the effort ought to be by force of public opinion to mitigate and assuage it. A fire not to be quenched, it demands a uniform vigilance to prevent its bursting into a flame, lest, instead of warming, it should consume.

It is important, likewise, that the habits of thinking in a free country should inspire caution in those intrusted with its administration to confine themselves within their respective constitutional spheres, avoiding in the exercise of the powers of one department to encroach upon another. The spirit of encroachment tends to consolidate the powers of all the departments in one, and thus to create, whatever the form of government, a real despotism. . . . If in the opinion of the people the distribution or modification of the constitutional powers be in any particular wrong, let it be corrected by an amendment in the way which the Constitution designates. But let there be no change by usurpation; for though this in one instance may be the instrument of good, it is the customary weapon by which free governments are destroyed. The precedent must always greatly overbalance in permanent evil any partial or transient benefit which the use can at any time yield.

Of all the dispositions and habits which lead to political prosperity, religion and morality are indispensable supports. In vain would that man claim the tribute of patriotism who should labor to subvert these great pillars of human happiness—these firmest props of the duties of men and citizens. The mere politician, equally with the pious man, ought to respect and to cherish them. A volume could not trace all their connections with private and public felicity. Let it simply be asked, Where is the security for property, for reputation, for life, if the sense of religious obligation *desert* the oaths which are the instruments of investigation in courts of justice? And let us with caution indulge the supposition that morality can be maintained without religion. Whatever may be conceded to the influence of refined education on minds of peculiar structure, reason and experience both forbid us to expect that national morality can prevail in exclusion of religious principle.

It is substantially true that virtue or morality is a necessary spring of popular government. The rule indeed extends with more or less force to every species of free government. Who that is a sincere friend to it can look with indifference upon attempts to shake the foundation of the fabric? Promote, then, as an object of primary importance, institutions for the general diffusion of knowledge. In proportion as the structure of a government gives force to public opinion, it is essential that public opinion should be enlightened.

As a very important source of strength and security, cherish public credit. One method of preserving it is to use it as sparingly as possible, avoiding occasions of expense by cultivating peace, but remembering also that timely disbursements to prepare for danger frequently prevent much greater disbursements to repel it; avoiding likewise the accumulation of debt, not only by shunning occasions of expense, but by vigorous exertions in time of peace to discharge the debts which unavoidable wars have occasioned, not ungenerously throwing upon posterity the burthen which we ourselves ought to bear. . . .

Observe good faith and justice toward all nations. Cultivate peace and harmony with all. Religion and morality enjoin this conduct. And can it be that good policy does not equally enjoin it? It will be worthy of a free, enlightened, and at no distant period a great nation to give to mankind the magnanimous and too novel example of a people always guided by an exalted justice and benevolence. Who can doubt that in the course of time and things the fruits of such a plan would richly repay any temporary advantages which might be lost by a steady adherence to it? Can it be that Providence has not connected the permanent felicity of a nation with its virtue? The experiment, at least, is recommended by every sentiment which ennobles human nature. Alas! is it rendered impossible by its vices?

In the execution of such a plan nothing is more essential than that permanent, inveterate antipathies against particular nations and passionate attachments for others should be excluded, and that in place of them just and amicable feelings toward all should be cultivated. The nation which indulges toward another an habitual hatred or an habitual fondness is in some degree a slave. It is a slave to its animosity or to its affection, either of which is sufficient to lead it astray from its duty and its interest. Antipathy in one nation against another disposes each more readily to offer insult and injury, to lay hold of slight causes of umbrage, and to be haughty and intractable when accidental or trifling occasions of dispute occur. . . .

So, likewise, a passionate attachment of one nation for another produces a variety of evils. Sympathy for the favorite nation, facilitating the illusion of an imaginary common interest in cases where no real common interest exists, and infusing into one the enmities of the other, betrays the former into a participation in the quarrels and wars of the latter without adequate inducement or justification. It leads also to concessions to the favorite nation of privileges denied to others, which is apt doubly to injure the nation making the concessions by unnecessarily parting with what ought to have been retained, and by exciting jealousy, ill will, and a disposition to retaliate in the parties from whom equal privileges are withheld; and it gives to ambitious, corrupted, or deluded citizens (who devote themselves to the favorite nation) facility to betray or sacrifice the interests of their own country without odium, sometimes even with popularity, gilding with the appearances of a virtuous sense of obligation, a commendable deference for public opinion, or a laudable zeal for public good the base or foolish compliances of ambition, corruption, or infatuation. . . .

Against the insidious wiles of foreign influence (I conjure you to believe me, fellow-citizens) the jealousy of a free people ought to be *constantly* awake, since history and experience prove that foreign influence is one of the most baneful foes of republican government. But that jealousy, to be useful, must be impartial, else it becomes the instrument of the very influence to be avoided, instead of a defense against it. Excessive partiality for one foreign nation and excessive dislike of another cause those whom they actuate to see danger only on one side, and serve to veil and even second the arts of influence on the other. Real patriots who may resist the intrigues of the favorite are liable to become suspected and odious, while its tools and dupes usurp the applause and confidence of the people to surrender their interests.

The great rule of conduct for us in regard to foreign nations is, in extending our commercial relations to have with them as little *political* connection as possible. So far as we have already formed engagements let them be fulfilled with perfect good faith. Here let us stop.

Europe has a set of primary interests which to us have none or a very remote relation. Hence she must be engaged in frequent controversies, the causes of which are essentially foreign to our concerns. Hence, therefore, it must be unwise in us to implicate ourselves by artificial ties in the ordinary vicissitudes of her politics or the ordinary combinations and collisions of her friendships or enmities.

Our detached and distant situation invites and enables us to pursue a different course. If we remain one people, under an efficient government, the period is not far off when we may defy material injury from external annoyance; when we may take such an attitude as will cause the neutrality we may at any time resolve upon to be scrupulously respected; when belligerent nations, under the impossibility of making acquisitions upon us, will not lightly hazard the giving us provocation; when we may choose peace or war, as our interest, guided by justice, shall counsel.

Why forego the advantages of so peculiar a situation? Why

quit our own to stand upon foreign ground? Why, by inter-
weaving our destiny with that of any part of Europe, entangle
our peace and prosperity in the toils of European ambition,
rivalship, interest, humor, or caprice?

It is our true policy to steer clear of permanent alliances
with any portion of the foreign world, so far, I mean, as we
are now at liberty to do it; for let me not be understood as
capable of patronizing infidelity to existing engagements. I
hold the maxim no less applicable to public than to private
affairs that honesty is always the best policy. I repeat, therefore, let those engagements be observed in their genuine
sense. But in my opinion it is unnecessary and would be unwise to extend them.

Taking care always to keep ourselves by suitable establishments on a respectable defensive posture, we may safely trust
to temporary alliances for extraordinary emergencies.

Harmony, liberal intercourse with all nations are recommended by policy, humanity, and interest. But even our commercial policy should hold an equal and impartial hand,
neither seeking nor granting exclusive favors or preferences;
consulting the natural course of things; diffusing and diver-
sifying by gentle means the streams of commerce, but forcing
nothing; establishing with powers so disposed, in order to
give trade a stable course, to define the rights of our mer-
chants, and to enable the Government to support them, con-
ventional rules of intercourse, the best that present circumstances and mutual opinion will permit, but temporary and
liable to be from time to time abandoned or varied as experience and circumstances shall dictate; constantly keeping
in view that it is folly in one nation to look for disinterested
favors from another; that it must pay with a portion of its
independence for whatever it may accept under that character;
that by such acceptance it may place itself in the condition
of having given equivalents for nominal favors, and yet of
being reproached with ingratitdde for not giving more. There
can be no greater error than to expect or calculate upon real

favors from nation to nation. It is an illusion which experience must cure, which a just pride ought to discard. . . .

Though in reviewing the incidents of my Administration I am unconscious of intentional error, I am nevertheless too sensible of my defects not to think it probable that I may have committed many errors. Whatever they may be, I fervently beseech the Almighty to avert or mitigate the evils to which they may tend. I shall also carry with me the hope that my country will never cease to view them with indulgence, and that, after forty-five years of my life dedicated to its service with an upright zeal, the faults of incompetent abilities will be consigned to oblivion, as myself must soon be to the mansions of rest.

Relying on its kindness in this as in other things, and actuated by that fervent love toward it which is so natural to a man who views in it the native soil of himself and his progenitors for several generations, I anticipate with pleasing expectation that retreat in which I promise myself to realize without alloy the sweet enjoyment of partaking in the midst of my fellow-citizens the benign influence of good laws under a free government—the ever-favorite object of my heart, and the happy reward, as I trust, of our mutual cares, labors, and dangers.

G⁰. Washington.

. . . this government,
the world's best hope . . .

FIRST INAUGURAL ADDRESS

By *Thomas Jefferson (1743–1826)*

JEFFERSON's diffidence and weak voice made him shy of appearances as a public speaker, but the occasion of his inauguration as President on March 4, 1801, called forth all his powers. His restatement of our national ideals in the face of the startling developments in international affairs which had taken place since 1789 is a valuable definition of Democracy. The triumph of Jefferson's Republican party seemed as ominous to many Americans of that time as the Revolution in France. The plea for political tolerance which this address contains was the President's answer to his opponents, but its influence has gone far beyond the immediate circumstances of its utterance. The success of our political institutions is based on the spirit which it expresses.

FRIENDS AND FELLOW CITIZENS: Called upon to undertake the duties of the first executive office of our country, I avail myself of the presence of that portion of my fellow-citizens which is here assembled, to express my grateful thanks for the favor with which they have been pleased to look toward me, to declare a sincere consciousness that the task is above my talents, and that I approach it with those anxious and awful presentiments, which the greatness of the charge, and the weakness of my powers, so justly inspire. A rising nation, spread over a wide and fruitful land, traversing all the seas with the rich productions of their industry, engaged in commerce with nations who feel power and forget right, advancing rapidly to destinies beyond the reach of mortal eye; when I contemplate these transcendent objects, and see the honor, the happiness, and the hopes of this beloved country committed to the issue and the auspices of this day, I shrink from the contemplation, and humble myself before the magnitude of the undertaking. Utterly, indeed, should I despair, did not the presence of many, whom I see here, remind me, that, in the other high authorities provided by our constitution, I shall find resources of wisdom, of virtue, and of zeal, on which to rely under all difficulties. To you, then, gentlemen, who are charged with the sovereign functions of legislation, and to those associated with you, I look with encouragement for that guidance and support which may enable us to steer with safety the vessel in which we are all embarked, amidst the conflicting elements of a troubled world.

During the contest of opinion through which we have passed, the animation of discussions and of exertions has sometimes worn an aspect which might impose on strangers unused to think freely, and to speak and to write what they think; but this being now decided by the voice of the nation, announced according to the rules of the constitution, all will of course arrange themselves under the will of the law, and unite in common efforts for the common good. All too will bear in mind this sacred principle, that though the will of the majority is in all cases to prevail, that will, to be rightful, must be reasonable; that the minority possess their equal rights, which equal laws must protect, and to violate which would be oppression. Let us then, fellow-citizens, unite with one heart and one mind, let us restore to social intercourse that harmony and affection without which liberty and even life itself are but dreary things. And let us reflect, that having banished from our land that religious intolerance under which mankind so long bled and suffered, we have yet gained little, if we countenance a political intolerance, as despotic, as wicked, and as capable of as bitter and bloody persecutions. During the throes and convulsions of the ancient world, during the agonizing spasms of infuriated man, seeking through blood and slaughter his long-lost liberty, it was not wonderful that the agitation of the billows should reach even this distant and peaceful shore; that this should be more felt and feared by some, and less by others, and should divide opinions as to measures of safety; but every difference of opinion is not a difference of principle. We have called by different names brethren of the same principle. We are all Republicans; we are all Federalists. If there be any among us who wish to dissolve this Union, or to change its republican form, let them stand undisturbed as monuments of the safety with which error of opinion may be tolerated, where reason is left free to combat it. I know, indeed, that some honest men fear that a republican government cannot be strong; that this government is not strong enough. But would the honest patriot, in the full tide of successful experiment, abandon a government which has so far kept us free and firm, on the theoretic and visionary fear, that this government, the world's best hope, may, by possibility, want energy to preserve itself? I trust not. I believe this, on the contrary, the strongest government on earth. I believe it the only one where every man, at the call of the law, would fly to the standard of the law, and would meet invasions of the public order as his own personal concern. Sometimes it is said that man cannot

be trusted with the government of himself. Can he then be
trusted with the government of others? Or, have we found
angels in the form of kings, to govern him? Let history answer this question.

Let us then, with courage and confidence, pursue our own
federal and republican principles; our attachment to union
and representative government. Kindly separated by nature
and a wide ocean from the exterminating havoc of one-
quarter of the globe; too high-minded to endure the degrada-
tion of the others, possessing a chosen country, with room
enough for our descendants to the thousandth and thousandth generation, entertaining a due sense of our equal
right to the use of our own faculties, to the acquisition of our
own industry, to honor and confidence from our fellow-citizens, resulting not from birth, but from our actions and their
sense of them, enlightened by a benign religion, professed
indeed and practised in various forms, yet all of them in-
culcating honesty, truth, temperance, gratitude, and the love
of man, acknowledging and adoring an overruling Providence, which, by all its dispensations, proves that it delights
in the happiness of man here, and his greater happiness
hereafter; with all these blessings, what more is necessary to
make us a happy and prosperous people? Still one thing
more, fellow-citizens, a wise and frugal government, which
shall restrain men from injuring one another, shall leave
them otherwise free to regulate their own pursuits of industry
and improvement, and shall not take from the mouth of labor
the bread it has earned. This is the sum of good government; and this is necessary to close the circle of our felicities.

About to enter, fellow-citizens, upon the exercise of duties
which comprehend everything dear and valuable to you, it is
proper you should understand what I deem the essential
principles of our government, and consequently, those which
ought to shape its administration. I will compress them
within the narrowest compass they will bear, stating the
general principle, but not all its limitations. Equal and exact
justice to all men, of whatever state or persuasion, religious

or political; peace, commerce, and honest friendship with all nations, entangling alliances with none; the support of the State governments in all their rights, as the most competent administrations for our domestic concerns, and the surest bulwarks against anti-republican tendencies; the preservation of the general government in its whole constitutional vigor, as the sheet-anchor of our peace at home and safety abroad; a jealous care of the right of election by the people, a mild and safe corrective of abuses which are lopped by the sword of revolution where peaceable remedies are unprovided; absolute acquiescence in the decisions of the majority, the vital principle of republics, from which there is no appeal but to force, the vital principle and immediate parent of despotism; a well-disciplined militia, our best reliance in peace, and for the first moments of war, till regulars may relieve them; the supremacy of the civil over the military authority; economy in the public expense, that labor may be lightly burdened; the honest payment of our debts, and sacred preservation of the public faith; encouragement of agriculture, and of commerce as its handmaid; the diffusion of information, and arraignment of all abuses at the bar of the public reason; freedom of religion, freedom of the press, and freedom of person, under the protection of the *habeas corpus,* and trial by juries impartially selected. These principles form the bright constellation, which has gone before us, and guided our steps through an age of revolution and reformation. The wisdom of our sages and blood of our heroes have been devoted to their attainment; they should be the creed of our political faith, the text of civic instruction, the touchstone by which to try the services of those we trust; and should we wander from them in moments of error or of alarm, let us hasten to retrace our steps, and to regain the road which alone leads to peace, liberty, and safety.

I repair, then, fellow-citizens, to the post you have assigned me. With experience enough in subordinate offices to have seen the difficulties of this, the greatest of all, I have learned to expect that it will rarely fall to the lot of imperfect man to retire from this station with the reputation and the favor which bring him into it. Without pretensions to that high confidence you reposed in our first and greatest revolutionary character, whose pre-eminent services had entitled him to the first place in his country's love, and destined for him the fairest page in the volume of faithful history, I ask so much confidence only as may give firmness and effect to the legal administration of your affairs. I shall often go wrong through defect of judgment. When right, I shall often be thought wrong by those whose positions will not command a view of the whole ground. I ask your indulgence for my own errors, which will never be intentional; and your support against the errors of others, who may condemn what they would not, if seen in all its parts. The approbation implied by your suffrage, is a great consolation to me for the past; and my future solicitude will be, to retain the good opinion of those who have bestowed it in advance, to conciliate that of others, by doing them all the good in my power, and to be instrumental to the happiness and freedom of all.

Relying then on the patronage of your good-will, I advance with obedience to the work, ready to retire from it whenever you become sensible how much better choices it is in your power to make. And may that infinite power which rules the destinies of the universe, lead our councils to what is best, and give them a favorable issue for your peace and prosperity.

Liberty and Union, now and forever, one
and inseparable.

From the REPLY TO HAYNE

By Daniel Webster (1782–1852)

DANIEL WEBSTER's masterpiece, often cited as the greatest oration
ever made in America, is more than a refutation of John C.
Calhoun's doctrine of nullification. It is an exposition of national ideals as they had developed by the year 1830. The parts of
the speech we present here show what the majority of Americans
had come to believe was the character of their Constitution and
of the Union it upheld. Senator Robert Hayne of South Carolina had maintained that the Constitution was a compact between sovereign States, each of which reserved the right to review
the laws of the national legislature, and, if necessary for the
sake of local justice, to nullify them. Webster replied that the
Constitution was an expression of assent to an already existing,
and henceforward indissoluble, Union. The powers granted
under the Constitution to the national government were to be
construed broadly, and only the Supreme Court might say
whether a law of the national government was, or was not, in ac-
cord with the Constitution.

THERE YET REMAINS to be performed, Mr. President, by far the most grave and important duty, which I feel to be devolved on me, by this occasion. It is to state, and to defend, what I conceive to be the true principles of the Constitution under which we are here assembled. I might well have desired that so weighty a task should have fallen into other and abler hands. I could have wished that it should have been executed by those whose character and experience give weight and influence to their opinions, such as can not possibly belong to mine. But, sir, I have met the occasion, not sought it: and I shall proceed to state my own sentiments, without challenging for them any particular regard, with studied plainness, and as much precision as possible.

I understand the honorable gentleman from South Carolina to maintain, that it is a right of the State legislatures to interfere, whenever, in their judgment, this government transcends its constitutional limits, and to arrest the operation of its laws.

I understand him to maintain this right, as a right existing under the Constitution, not as a right to overthrow it on the ground of extreme necessity, such as would justify violent revolution.

I understand him to maintain an authority on the part of the States thus to interfere for the purpose of correcting the exercise of power by the general government, of checking it, and of compelling it to conform to their opinion of the extent of its powers.

I understand him to maintain that the ultimate power of judging of the constitutional extent of its own authority is not lodged exclusively in the general government, or any branch of it; but that, on the contrary, the States may lawfully decide for themselves, and each State for itself, whether in a given case the act of the general government transcends its power.

I understand him to insist that if the exigency of the case, ın the opinion of any State government, require it, such State government may, by its own sovereign authority, annul an act of the general government which it deems plainly and palpably unconstitutional.

This is the sum of what I understand from him to be the South Carolina doctrine, and the doctrine which he maintains. I propose to consider it, and compare it with the Constitution. Allow me to say, as a preliminary remark, that I call this the South Carolina doctrine only because the gentleman himself has so denominated it. I do not feel at liberty to say that South Carolina, as a State, has ever advanced these sentiments. I hope she has not, and never may. That a great majority of her people are opposed to the tariff laws, is doubtless true. That a majority somewhat less than that just mentioned, conscientiously believe these laws unconstitutional, may probably also be true. But that any majority holds to the right of direct State interference, at State discretion,— the right of nullifying acts of Congress by acts of State legislation,—is more than I know, and what I shall be slow to believe. . . .

What he contends for is, that it is constitutional to interrupt the administration of the Constitution itself, in the hands of those who are chosen and sworn to administer it, by the direct interference, in form of law, of the State, in virtue of their sovereign capacity. The inherent right in the people to reform the government I do not deny: and they have another right, and that is, to resist unconstitutional laws without overturning the government. It is no doctrine of mine that unconstitutional laws bind the people. The great question is, whose prerogative is it to decide on the constitutionality or unconstitutionality of the laws? On that the main debate hinges. The proposition that, in case of a supposed violation of the Constitution by Congress, the States have a constitutional right to interfere and annul the law of Congress, is the proposition of the gentleman: I do not admit it. If the gentleman had intended no more than to assert the right of revolution for justifiable cause, he would have said only what all agree to. But I can not conceive that there can be a middle course between submission to the laws when regularly pronounced constitutional, on the one hand, and open resistance,—which is revolution, or rebellion,—on the other. I say, the right of a State to annul a law of Congress can not be maintained but on the ground of the unalienable right of man to resist oppression; that is to say, upon the ground of revolution. I admit that there is an ultimate violent remedy, above the Constitution and in defiance of the Constitution, which may be resorted to when a revolution is to be justified. But I do not admit that, under the Constitution, and in conformity with it, there is any mode in which a State government, as a member of the Union, can interfere and stop the progress of the general government, by force of her own laws, under any circumstances whatever.

This leads us to inquire into the origin of this government, and the source of its power. Whose agent is it? Is it the creature of the State legislatures, or the creature of the people? If the government of the United States be the agent of the State governments, then they may control it, provided they can agree in the manner of controlling it; if it be the agent of the people, then the people alone can control it, restrain it, modify or reform it. It is observable enough, that the doctrine for which the honorable gentleman contends, leads him to the necessity of maintaining, not only that this general government is the creature of the States, but that it is the creature of each of the States severally; so that each may assert the power, for itself, of determining whether it acts within the limits of its authority. It is the servant of four and twenty masters, of different wills and different purposes, and yet bound to obey all. This absurdity (for it seems no less) arises from a misconception as to the origin of this government and its true character. It is, sir, the people's Constitution, the people's government; made for the people; made by the people; and answerable to the people. The people of the United States have declared that this Constitution shall be the supreme law. We must either admit the proposition, or dispute their authority. The States are, unquestionably, sovereign so far as their sovereignty is not affected by this supreme law. But the State legislatures as political bodies, however sovereign, are yet not sovereign over the people. So far as the people have given power to the general government, so far the grant is unquestionably good, and the government holds of the people and not of the State governments. We are all agents of the same supreme power, the people. The general government and the State governments derive their authority from the same source. Neither can, in relation to the other, be called primary, though one is definite and restricted and the other general and residuary. The national government possesses those powers which it can be shown the people have conferred on it, and no more. All the rest belongs to the State governments or to the people themselves. So far as the people have restrained State sovereignty, by the expression of their will in the Constitution of the United States, so far it must be admitted State sovereignty is effectually controlled. I do not contend that it is, or ought to be, controlled farther. The sentiment to which I have referred propones that State sovereignty is only to be controlled by its own "feeling of justice:" that is to say, it is not to be controlled at all; for one who is to follow his own feelings is under no legal control. Now, however men may think this ought to be, the fact is that the people of the United States have chosen to impose control on State sovereignties. There are those, doubtless, who wish they had been left without restraint; but the Constitution has ordered the matter differently. To make war, for instance, is an exercise of sovereignty; but the Constitution declares that no State shall make war. To coin money is another exercise of sovereign power; but no State is at liberty to coin money. Again, the Constitution says that no sovereign State shall be so sovereign as to make a treaty. These prohibitions, it must be confessed, are a control on the State sovereignty of South Carolina, as well as of the other States, which does not arise "from her own feelings of honorable justice." Such an opinion, therefore, is in defiance of the plainest provisions of the Constitution. . . .

In Carolina the tariff is a palpable, deliberate usurpation; Carolina, therefore, may nullify it, and refuse to pay the duties. In Pennsylvania it is both clearly constitutional and highly expedient; and there the duties are to be paid. And yet we live under a government of uniform laws, and under a Constitution, too, which contains an express provision, as it happens, that all duties shall be equal in all the States. Does not this approach absurdity?

If there be no power to settle such questions, independent of either of the States, is not the whole Union a rope of sand? Are we not thrown back again precisely upon the old Confederation?

It is too plain to be argued. Four and twenty interpreters of constitutional law, each with a power to decide for itself, and none with authority to bind anybody else, and this constitutional law the only bond of their Union! What is such a state of things but a mere connection during pleasure or, to use the phraseology of the times, during feeling? And that feeling, too, not the feeling of the people, who established the Constitution, but the feeling of the State governments. . . .

I must now beg to ask, sir, whence is this supposed right of the States derived?—where do they find the power to interfere with the laws of the Union? Sir, the opinion which the honorable gentleman maintains is a notion, founded in a total misapprehension, in my judgment, of the origin of this government, and of the foundation on which it stands. I hold it to be a popular government, erected by the people; those who administer it, responsible to the people; and itself capable of being amended and modified, just as the people may choose it should be. It is as popular, just as truly emanating from the people, as the State governments. It is created for one purpose; the State governments for another. It has its own powers; they have theirs. There is no more authority with them to arrest the operation of a law of Congress, than with Congress to arrest the operation of their laws. We are here to administer a Constitution emanating immediately from the people, and trusted by them to our administration. It is not the creature of the State governments. It is of no moment to the argument, that certain acts of the State legislatures are necessary to fill our seats in this body. That is not one of their original State powers, a part of the sovereignty of the State. It is a duty which the people, by the Constitution itself, have imposed on the State legislatures; and which they might have left to be performed elsewhere, if they had seen fit. So they have left the choice of President with electors; but all this does not affect the proposition, that this whole government—President, Senate, and House of Representatives—is a popular government. It leaves it still all its popular character. The governor of a State (in some of the States) is chosen, not directly by the people, but by those who are chosen by the people, for the purpose of performing among other duties that of electing a governor. Is the government of the State, on that account, not a popular government? This government, sir, is the independent offspring of the popular will. It is not the creature of State legislatures; nay, more, if the whole truth must be told, the people brought it into existence, established it, and have hitherto supported it, for the very purpose, amongst others, of imposing certain salutary restraints on State sovereignties. The States can not now make war; they can not contract alliances; they can not make, each for itself, separate regulations of commerce; they can not lay imposts; they can not coin money. If this Constitution, sir, be the creature of State legislatures, it must be admitted that it has obtained a strange control over the volitions of its creators.

The people then, sir, erected this government. They gave it a Constitution, and in that Constitution they have enumerated the powers which they bestow on it. They have made it a limited government. They have defined its authority. They have restrained it to the exercise of such powers as are granted; and all others, they declare, are reserved to the States, or the people. But, sir, they have not stopped here. If they had, they would have accomplished but half their work. No definition can be so clear, as to avoid possibility of doubt; no limitation so precise, as to exclude all uncertainty. Who, then, shall construe this grant of the people? Who shall interpret their will, where it may be supposed they have left it doubtful? With whom do they repose this ultimate right of deciding on the powers of the government? Sir, they have settled all this in the fullest manner. They have left it with the goverment itself, in its appropriate branches. Sir, the very chief end, the main design, for which the whole Constitution was framed and adopted, was to establish a government that should not be obliged to act through State agency, or depend on State opinion and State discretion. The people had had quite enough of that kind of government, under the Confederacy. Under that system, the legal action—the application of law to individuals —belonged exclusively to the States. Congress could only recommend—their acts were not of binding force till the States had adopted and sanctioned them. Are we in that condition still? Are we yet at the mercy of State discretion, and State construction? Sir, if we are, then vain will be our attempt to maintain the Constitution under which we sit.

But, sir, the people have wisely provided, in the Constitution itself, a proper, suitable mode and tribunal for settling questions of constitutional law. There are, in the Constitution, grants of powers to Congress; and restrictions on these powers. There are, also, prohibitions on the States. Some authority must, therefore, necessarily exist, having the ultimate jurisdiction to fix and ascertain the interpretation of these grants, restrictions, and prohibitions. The Constitution has itself pointed out, ordained, and established that authority. How has it accomplished this great and essential end? By declaring, sir, that "the Constitution and the laws of the United States, made in pursuance thereof, shall be the supreme law of the land, anything in the constitution or laws of any State to the contrary notwithstanding."

This, sir, was the first great step. By this the supremacy of the Constitution and laws of the United States is declared. The people so will it. No State law is to be valid, which comes in conflict with the Constitution, or any law of the United States passed in pursuance of it. But who shall decide this question of interference? To whom lies the last appeal? This, sir, the Constitution itself decides, also, by declaring, "that the judicial power shall extend to all cases arising under the Constitution and laws of the United States." These two provisions, sir, cover the whole ground. They are, in truth, the keystone of the arch. With these it is a constitution; without them it is a confederacy. In pursuance of these clear and express provisions, Congress established, at its very first session, in the judicial act, a mode for carrying them into full effect, and for bringing all questions of constitutional power to the final decision of the Supreme Court. It then, sir, became a government. It then had the means of self-protection; and, but for this, it would, in all probability, have been now among things which are past. Having constituted the government, and declared its powers, the people have further said, that since somebody must decide on the extent of these powers, the government shall itself decide; subject, always, like other popular governments, to its responsibility to the people. And now, sir, I repeat, how is it that a State legislature acquires any power to interfere? Who, or what, gives them the right to say to the people, "We, who are your agents and servants for one purpose, will undertake to decide that your other agents and servants, appointed by you for another purpose have transcended the authority you gave them!" The reply would be, I think, not impertinent: "Who made you a judge over another's servants? To their own masters they stand or fall.". . .

The honorable gentleman argues, that if this government be the sole judge of the extent of its own powers, whether that right of judging be in Congress or the Supreme Court, it equally subverts State sovereignty. This the gentleman sees, or thinks he sees, although he can not perceive how the right of judging in this matter, if left to the exercise of State legislatures, has any tendency to subvert the government of the Union. The gentleman's opinion may be that the right ought not to have been lodged with the general government; he may like better such a constitution as we should have under the right of State interference: but I ask him to meet me on the plain matter of fact; I ask him to meet me on the Constitution itself; I ask him if the power is not found there—clearly and visibly found there? . . .

If anything be found in the national Constitution, either by original provision or subsequent interpretation, which ought not to be in it, the people know how to get rid of it. If any construction be established unacceptable to them, so as to become practically a part of the Constitution, they will amend it at their own sovereign pleasure: but while the people choose to maintain it as it is,—while they are satisfied with it and refuse to change it,—who has given, or who can give, to the State legislatures a right to alter it, either by interference, construction, or otherwise? Gentlemen do not seem to recollect that the people have any power to do anything for themselves; they imagine there is no safety for them, any longer than they are under the close guardianship of the State legislatures. Sir, the people have not trusted their safety, in regard to the general Constitution, to these hands. They have required other security, and taken other bonds. They have chosen to trust themselves, first, to the plain words of the instrument, and to such construction as the government itself, in doubtful cases, should put on its own powers, under their oaths of office and subject to their responsibility to them: just as the people of a State trust their own State governments with a similar power. Secondly, they have reposed their trust in the efficacy of frequent elections, and in their own power to remove their own servants and agents, whenever they see cause. Thirdly, they have reposed trust in the judicial power, which in order that it might be trustworthy, they have made as respectable, as disinterested, and as independent as was practicable. Fourthly, they have seen fit to rely, in case of necessity or high expediency, on their known and admitted power to alter or amend the Constitution, peaceably and quietly, whenever experience shall point out defects or imperfections. And finally, the people of the United States have at no time, in no way, directly or indirectly, authorized any State legislature to construe or interpret their high instrument of government; much less to interfere, by their own power, to arrest its course and operation.

If, sir, the people, in these respects, had done otherwise than they have done, their Constitution could neither have been preserved, nor would it have been worth preserving. And if its plain provisions shall now be disregarded, and these new doctrines interpolated in it, it will become as feeble and helpless a being as its enemies, whether early or more recent, could possibly desire. It will exist in every State, but as a poor dependent on State permission. It must borrow leave to be; and *will* be no longer than State pleasure, or State discretion, sees fit to grant the indulgence and to prolong its poor existence.

But, sir, although there are fears, there are hopes also. The people have preserved this, their own chosen Constitution, for forty years, and have seen their happiness, prosperity, and renown, grow with its growth, and strengthen with its strength. They are now, generally, strongly attached to it. Overthrown by direct assault, it can not be; evaded, undermined, nullified, it will not be, if we, and those who shall succeed us here as agents and representatives of the people, shall conscientiously and vigilantly discharge the two great branches of our public trust—faithfully to preserve and wisely to administer it.

Mr. President, I have thus stated the reasons of my dissent to the doctrines which have been advanced and maintained. I am conscious of having detained you and the Senate much too long. I was drawn into the debate, with no previous deliberation such as is suited to the discussion of so grave and important a subject. But it is a subject of which my heart is full, and I have not been willing to suppress the utterance of its spontaneous sentiments. I can not, even now, persuade myself to relinquish it without expressing once more my deep conviction that, since it respects nothing less than the union of the States, it is of most vital and essential importance to the public happiness. I profess, sir, in my career hitherto to have kept steadily in view the prosperity and honor of the whole country, and the preservation of our Federal Union. It is to that Union we owe our safety at home, and our consideration and dignity abroad. . . .

While the Union lasts, we have high, exciting, gratifying prospects spread out before us, for us and our children. Beyond that I seek not to penetrate the veil. God grant that, in my day at least, that curtain may not rise. God grant, that on my vision never may be opened what lies behind. When my eyes shall be turned to behold, for the last time, the sun in heaven, may I not see him shining on the broken and dishonored fragments of a once glorious Union; on States dissevered, discordant, belligerent; on a land rent with civil feuds, or drenched, it may be, in fraternal blood! Let their last feeble and lingering glance rather behold the gorgeous ensign of the republic, now known and honored throughout the earth, still full high advanced, its arms and trophies streaming in their original luster, not a stripe erased or polluted, nor a single star obscured—bearing for its motto, no such miserable interrogatory as, What is all this worth? Nor those other words of delusion and folly, Liberty first, and Union afterwards—but everywhere, spread all over in characters of living light, blazing on all its ample folds, as they float over the sea and over the land, and in every wind under the whole heavens, that other sentiment, dear to every true American heart—Liberty and Union, now and forever, one and inseparable!

Are we to sell reality for a phantom?

ADDRESS
AT THE UNION MASS MEETING,
AUSTIN, TEXAS

By Sam Houston (1793–1863)

SAM HOUSTON spoke seldom in Congress, and sometimes with a careless lack of preparation, but whenever he raised his voice in defense of the rights of the Indians or in defense of the Union, he was truly eloquent. After the great days in which he helped win the independence of Texas and saw her become a State, he became an increasingly lonely figure among his Southern associates. He voted for the admission of Oregon as a free State, and for all the compromise measures of 1850, stoutly maintaining that he made no distinction between North or South—that rights were not the property of any State but common to the whole Union. Although the tide was running against him, even in his own Texas, he continued to stand by his principles. The following speech, made on September 22, 1860, is one of the most interesting of his statements on policy.

LADIES AND FELLOW-CITIZENS: I had looked forward and with many pleasing anticipations to this occasion, as I always do to a meeting with my fellow-citizens, hoping that no untoward circumstance would arise to prevent my giving full utterance to my sentiments on the political topics of the day; but ill-health has overtaken me, and I have against the advice of my physician, arisen from a sick-bed to make my apology for not being able to fill my appointment; but being here, I will endeavor to say a few words in behalf of the Union, and the necessity of union to preserve it, which I trust will not fall unheeded. The condition of the country is such, the dangers which beset it are so numerous, the foes of the Union so implacable and energetic, that no risk should be heeded by him who has a voice to raise in its behalf; and so long as I have strength to stand, I will peril even health in its cause.

I had felt an interest in this occasion, on many accounts. It is said a crisis is impending. The clamor of disunion is heard in the land. The safety of the Government is threatened; and it seemed to me that the time had come for a renewal of our vows of fidelity to the Constitution and to interchange, one with the other, sentiments of devotion to the whole country. I begin to feel that the issue really is upon us, which involves the perpetuity of the Government which we have received from our fathers. Were we to fail to pay our tributes to its worth, and to enlist in its defense, we would be unworthy longer to enjoy it.

It has been my misfortune to peril my all for the Union. So indissolubly connected is my life, my history, my hopes, my fortunes, with it, that when it falls, I would ask that with it might close my career, that I might not survive the destruction of the shrine that I had been taught to regard as holy and inviolate, since my boyhood. I have beheld it, the fairest fabric of Government God ever vouchsafed to man, more than a half century. May it never be my fate to stand sadly

70

gazing on its ruins! To be deprived of it, after enjoying it so long, would be a calamity, such as no people yet have endured.

Upwards of forty-seven years ago, I enlisted, a mere boy, to sustain the National flag and in defense of a harassed frontier, now the abode of a dense civilization. Then disunion was never heard of, save a few discordant notes from the Hartford Convention. It was anathematized by every patriot in the land, and the concocters of the scheme were branded as traitors. The peril I then underwent, in common with my fellow-soldiers, in behalf of the Union, would have been in vain, unless the patriotism of the nation had arisen against these disturbers of the public peace. With what heart could these gallant men again volunteer in defense of the Union, unless the Union could withstand the shock of treason and overturn the traitors? It did this; and when again, in 1836, I volunteered to aid in transplanting American liberty to this soil, it was with the belief that the Constitution and the Union were to be perpetual blessings to the human race,— that the success of the experiment of our fathers was beyond dispute, and that whether under the banner of the Lone Star or that many-starred banner of the Union, I could point to the land of Washington, Jefferson, and Jackson, as the land blest beyond all other lands, where freedom would be eternal and Union unbroken. It concerns me deeply, as it does every one here, that these bright anticipations should be realized; and that it should be continued not only the proudest nationality the world has ever produced, but the freest and the most perfect. I have seen it extend from the wilds of Tennessee, then a wilderness, across the Mississippi, achieve the annexation of Texas, scaling the Rocky Mountains in its onward march, sweeping the valleys of California, and laving its pioneer footsteps in the waves of the Pacific. I have seen this mighty progress, and it still remains free and independent. Power, wealth, expansion, victory, have followed in its path, and yet the ægis of the Union has been broad enough to encompass all. Is not this worth perpetuating? Will you exchange this for all the hazards, the anarchy and carnage of civil war? Do you believe that it will be dissevered and no shock felt in society? You are asked to plunge into a revolution; but are you told how to get out of it? Not so; but it is to be a leap in the dark—a leap into an abyss, whose horrors would even fright the mad spirits of disunion who tempt you on.

Our forefathers saw the danger to which freedom would be subjected, from the helpless condition of disunited States; and, to "form a more perfect Union," they established this Government. They saw the effect of foreign influence on rival States, the effect of dissensions at home, and to strengthen all and perpetuate all, to bind all together, yet leave all free, they gave us the Constitution and the Union. Where are the evidences that their patriotic labor was in vain? Have we not emerged from an infant's to a giant's strength? Have not empires been added to our domain, and States been created? All the blessings which they promised their posterity have been vouchsafed; and millions now enjoy them, who without this Union would to-day be oppressed and down-trodden in far-off foreign lands!

What is there that is free that we have not? Are our rights invaded and no Government ready to protect them? No! Are our institutions wrested from us and others foreign to our taste forced upon us? No! Is the right of free speech, a free press, or free suffrage taken from us? No! Has our property been taken from us and the Government failed to interpose when called upon? No, none of these! The rights of the States and the rights of individuals are still maintained. We have yet the Constitution, we have yet a judiciary, which has never been appealed to in vain—we have yet just laws and officers to administer them; and an army and navy, ready to maintain any and every constitutional right of the citizen. Whence then this clamor about disunion? Whence this cry of protection to property or disunion, when even the very loudest in the cry, declared under their Senatorial oaths,

but a few months since, that no protection was necessary?
Are we to sell reality for a phantom? . . .

It is but natural that we all should desire the defeat of
the Black Republican candidates. As Southern men, the
fact that their party is based upon the one idea of opposition
to our institutions, is enough to demand our efforts against
them; but we have a broader, a more national cause of opposition to them. Their party is sectional. It is at war with
those principles of equality and nationality upon which the
Government is formed, and as much the foe of the Northern
as of the Southern man. Its mission is to engender strife, to
foster hatred between brethren, and to encourage the formation here of Southern sectional parties equally dangerous to
Southern and Northern rights. The conservative energies of
the country are called upon to take a stand now against the
Northern sectional party, because its strength betokens success. Defeat and overthrow it, and the defeat and overthrow
of Southern sectionalism is easy.

I come not here to speak in behalf of a united South
against Lincoln. I appeal to the nation. I ask not the defeat
of sectionalism by sectionalism, but by nationality. These men
who talk of a united South, know well that it begets a united
North. Talk of frightening the North into measures by
threats of dissolving the Union! It is child's play and folly.
It is all the Black Republican leaders want. American blood,
North nor South, has not yet become so ignoble as to be
chilled by threats. Strife begets strife, threat begets threat,
and taunt begets taunt, and these disunionists know it. American blood brooks no such restraints as these men would put
upon it. I would blush with shame for America, if I could
believe that one vast portion of my countrymen had sunk so
low that childish threats would intimidate them. . . . No,
these are not the arguments to use. I would appeal rather to
the great soul of the nation than to the passions of a section.
I would say to Northern as well as Southern men, "Here is a
party inimical to the rights of the whole country, such a party

as Washington warned us against. Let us put it down"; and this is the only way it can be put down.

The error has been that the South has met sectionalism by sectionalism. We want a Union basis, one broad enough to comprehend the good and true friends of the Constitution at the North. To hear Southern disunionists talk, you would think the majority of the Northern people were in this Black Republican party; but it is not so. They are in a minority, and it but needs a patriotic movement like that supported by the conservatives of Texas, to unite the divided opposition to that party there and overthrow it. Why, in New York, Pennsylvania, and New Jersey alone, the conservatives had a majority of over 250,000 at the last Presidential election, and in the entire North a majority of about 270,000. Because a minority at the North are inimical to us, shall we cut loose from the majority, or shall we not rather encourage the majority to unite and aid us?

I came not here to vindicate candidates or denounce them. They stand upon their records. If they are national, approve them; if they are sectional, condemn. Judge them by the principles they announce. Let past differences be forgotten in the determination to unite against sectionalism. I have differed with all three of the candidates; but whenever I see a man at this crisis coming boldly up to the defense of the Constitution of the country, and ready to maintain the Union against its foes, I will not permit old scores to prejudice me against him. Hence I am ready to vote the Union ticket, and if all the candidates occupy this national ground, my vote may be transferred to either of them. This is the way to put Mr. Lincoln down. Put him down constitutionally, by rallying the conservative forces and sacrificing men for the sake of principles.

But if, through division in the ranks of those opposed to Mr. Lincoln, he should be elected, we have no excuse for dissolving the Union. The Union is worth more than Mr. Lincoln, and if the battle is to be fought for the Constitution, let us fight it in the Union and for the sake of the Union.

With a majority of the people in favor of the Constitution, shall we desert the Government and leave it in the hands of the minority? A new obligation will be imposed upon us, to guard the Constitution and to see that no infraction of it is attempted or permitted. If Mr. Lincoln administers the Government in accordance with the Constitution, our rights must be respected. If he does not, the Constitution has provided a remedy. . . .

These are no new sentiments to me. I uttered them in the American Senate in 1856. I utter them now. I was denounced then as a traitor. I am denounced now. Be it so! Men who never endured the privation, the toil, the peril that I have for my country, call me a traitor because I am willing to yield obedience to the Constitution and the constituted authorities. Let them suffer what I have for this Union, and they will feel it entwining so closely around their hearts that it will be like snapping the cords of life to give it up. Let them learn to respect and support one Government before they talk of starting another. I have been taught to believe that plotting the destruction of the Government is treason; but these gentlemen call a man a traitor because he desires to sustain the Government and to uphold the Constitution. . . .

I can speak but little longer; but let my last words be remembered by you. When I look back and remember the names which are canonized as the tutelar saints of liberty, and the warnings they have given you against disunion, I can not believe that you will be led astray. I can not be long among you. My sands of life are fast running out. As the glass becomes exhausted, if I can feel that I leave my country prosperous and united, I shall die content. To leave men with whom I have mingled in troublous times, and whom I have learned to love as brothers—to leave the children of those whom I have seen pass away, after lives of devotion to the Union—to leave the people who have borne me up and sustained me—to leave my country, and not feel that the liberty and happiness I have enjoyed would still be theirs, would be the worst pang of death. I am to leave children among you to share the fate of your children. Think you I feel no interest in the future for their sakes? We are passing away. They must encounter the evils that are to come. In the far distant future, the generations that spring from our loins are to venture in the path of glory and honor. If untrammeled, who can tell the mighty progress they will make? If cast adrift—if the calamitous curse of disunion is inflicted upon them, who can picture their misfortunes and shame?

*. . . that this nation, under God, shall have
a new birth of freedom . . .*

THE GETTYSBURG ADDRESS

By Abraham Lincoln (1809–1865)

EDWARD EVERETT's eloquent and polished address at the dedication of the cemetery at Gettysburg on November 19, 1863, lasted two full hours. The assemblage who listened, probably assuming that President Lincoln was present as a mere figurehead, could not have realized that his words—and not those of the principal orator—were to carry the concentrated thought of the occasion to farthest posterity.

Perhaps never, since man became articulate, has a speech more brilliantly crystallized lofty and "altogether fitting" sentiments than have these 266 words.

FOURSCORE AND SEVEN YEARS ago our fathers brought forth on this continent a new nation, conceived in Liberty, and dedicated to the proposition that all men are created equal.

Now we are engaged in a great civil war, testing whether that nation, or any nation so conceived and so dedicated, can long endure. We are met on a great battlefield of that war. We have come to dedicate a portion of that field, as a final resting-place for those who here gave their lives that that nation might live. It is altogether fitting and proper that we should do this.

But, in a larger sense, we cannot dedicate—we cannot consecrate—we cannot hallow—this ground. The brave men, living and dead, who struggled here, have consecrated it far above our poor power to add or detract. The world will little note nor long remember what we say here, but it can never forget what they did here. It is for us, the living, rather, to be dedicated here to the unfinished work which they who fought here have thus far so nobly advanced. It is rather for us to be here dedicated to the great task remaining before us—that from these honored dead we take increased devotion to that cause for which they gave the last full measure of devotion; that we here highly resolve that these dead shall not have died in vain; that this nation, under God, shall have a new birth of freedom; and that government of the people, by the people, for the people, shall not perish from the earth.

With malice toward none . . .

SECOND INAUGURAL ADDRESS WASHINGTON, D.C., MARCH 4, 1865

By Abraham Lincoln

A SPEECH could hardly be more self-explanatory than this one. Lincoln's words, brief and cogent as usual, clearly revealed the occasion, its background, and its great central theme of hope for universal peace and charity. The final paragraph is at once a lasting memorial to, and a perfect portrait of, Lincoln's great soul.

Lincoln himself realized what an excellent speech he had made. "I expect it," he said, "to wear as well as, perhaps better than, anything I have produced."

FELLOW-COUNTRYMEN: At this second appearing to take the oath of the presidential office, there is less occasion for an extended address than there was at the first. Then a statement, somewhat in detail, of a course to be pursued, seemed fitting and proper. Now, at the expiration of four years, during which public declarations have been constantly called forth on every point and phase of the great contest which still absorbs the attention and engrosses the energies of the nation, little that is new could be presented. The progress of our arms, upon which all else chiefly depends, is as well known to the public as to myself; and it is, I trust, reasonably satisfactory and encouraging to all. With high hope for the future, no prediction in regard to it is ventured.

On the occasion corresponding to this four years ago, all thoughts were anxiously directed to an impending civil war. All dreaded it—all sought to avert it. While the inaugural address was being delivered from this place, devoted altogether to saving the Union without war, insurgent agents were in the city seeking to destroy it without war—seeking to dissolve the Union, and divide effects, by negotiation. Both parties deprecated war; but one of them would make war rather than let the nation survive; and the other would accept war rather than let it perish. And the war came.

One-eighth of the whole population were colored slaves, not distributed generally over the Union, but localized in the Southern part of it. These slaves constituted a peculiar and powerful interest. All knew that this interest was, somehow, the cause of the war. To strengthen, perpetuate, and extend this interest was the object for which the insurgents would rend the Union, even by war; while the government claimed no right to do more than to restrict the territorial enlargement of it.

Neither party expected for the war the magnitude or the duration which it has already attained. Neither anticipated that the cause of the conflict might cease with, or even before, the conflict itself should cease. Each looked for an easier triumph, and a result less fundamental and astounding. Both read the same Bible, and pray to the same God; and each invokes His aid against the other. It may seem strange that any men should dare to ask a just God's assistance in wringing their bread from the sweat of other men's faces; but let us judge not, that we be not judged. The prayers of both could not be answered—that of neither has been answered fully.

The Almighty has His own purposes. "Woe unto the world because of offenses! for it must needs be that offenses come; but woe to that man by whom the offense cometh." If we shall suppose that American slavery is one of those offenses which, in the providence of God, must needs come, but which, having continued through His appointed time, He now wills to remove, and that He gives to both North and South this terrible war, as the woe due to those by whom the offense came, shall we discern therein any departure from those divine attributes which the believers in a living God always ascribe to Him? Fondly do we hope—fervently do we pray—that this mighty scourge of war may speedily pass away. Yet, if God wills that it continue until all the wealth piled by the bondman's two hundred and fifty years of unrequited toil shall be sunk, and until every drop of blood drawn with the lash shall be paid by another drawn with the sword, as was said three thousand years ago, so still it must be said, "The judgments of the Lord are true and righteous altogether."

With malice toward none; with charity for all; with firmness in the right, as God gives us to see the right, let us strive on to finish the work we are in; to bind up the nation's wounds; to care for him who shall have borne the battle, and for his widow, and his orphan—to do all which may achieve and cherish a just and lasting peace among ourselves, and with all nations.

We have no higher duty than to promote
the efficiency of the individual.

A CHARTER OF DEMOCRACY

By Theodore Roosevelt (1858–1919)

THIS ADDRESS was delivered at Columbus, Ohio, on February 21, 1912, before a convention which was engaged in preparing a new Constitution for that State. A few days later, "TR" tossed his hat in the ring and began an aggressive campaign to capture the Republican nomination for the Presidency—an effort which wound up in the creation of the Progressive party and Taft's defeat in the fall election. Aside from its political interest, it is an excellent statement of Theodore Roosevelt's thought on constitutional questions and of his concept of Democracy. The latter half of the address, devoted to specific methods of reform, has been deleted.

. . . I BELIEVE in pure democracy. With Lincoln, I hold that "this country, with its institutions, belongs to the people who inhabit it. Whenever they shall grow weary of the existing government, they can exercise their constitutional right of amending it."

We Progressives believe that the people have the right, the power, and the duty to protect themselves and their own welfare; that human rights are supreme over all other rights; that wealth should be the servant, not the master, of the people.

We believe that unless representative government does absolutely represent the people it is not representative government at all.

We test the worth of all men and all measures by asking how they contribute to the welfare of the men, women, and children of whom this nation is composed.

We are engaged in one of the great battles of the age-long contest waged against privilege on behalf of the common welfare.

We hold it a prime duty of the people to free our government from the control of money in politics.

For this purpose we advocate, not as ends in themselves, but as weapons in the hands of the people, all governmental devices which will make the representatives of the people more easily and certainly responsible to the people's will.

This country, as Lincoln said, belongs to the people. So do the natural resources which make it rich. They supply the basis of our prosperity now and hereafter. In preserving them, which is a national duty, we must not forget that monopoly is based on the control of natural resources and natural advantages, and that it will help the people little to conserve our natural wealth unless the benefits which it can yield are secured to the people.

Let us remember, also, that conservation does not stop with the natural resources, but that the principle of making the best use of all we have requires with equal or greater in-

sistence that we shall stop the waste of human life in industry
and prevent the waste of human welfare which flows from
the unfair use of concentrated power and wealth in the hands
of men whose eagerness for profit blinds them to the cost of
what they do.

We have no higher duty than to promote the efficiency of
the individual. There is no surer road to the efficiency of the
nation.

I am emphatically a believer in constitutionalism, and because of this fact I no less emphatically protest against any
theory that would make of the constitution a means of thwart-
ing instead of securing the absolute right of the people to rule
themselves and to provide for their social and industrial well-
being.

All constitutions, those of the States no less than that of the
nation, are designed, and must be interpreted and administered so as to fit human rights.

Lincoln so interpreted and administered the National Constitution. Buchanan attempted the reverse, attempted to fit
human rights to, and limit them by, the Constitution. It was
Buchanan who treated the courts as a fetich, who protested
against and condemned all criticism of the judges for unjust
and unrighteous decisions, and upheld the Constitution as
an instrument for the protection of privilege and of vested
wrong. It was Lincoln who appealed to the people against
the judges when the judges went wrong, who advocated and
secured what was practically the recall of the Dred Scott decision, and who treated the Constitution as a living force for
righteousness.

We stand for applying the Constitution to the issues of to-
day as Lincoln applied it to the issues of his day; Lincoln,
mind you, and not Buchanan, was the real upholder and
preserver of the Constitution, for the true Progressive, the
Progressive of the Lincoln stamp, is the only true constitu-
tionalist, the only real conservative.

The object of every American constitution worth calling
such must be what it is set forth to be in the preamble to the

National Constitution, "to establish justice," that is, to secure justice as between man and man by means of genuine popular self-government. If the constitution is successfully invoked to nullify the effort to remedy injustice, it is proof positive either that the constitution needs immediate amendment or else that it is being wrongfully and improperly construed.

I therefore very earnestly ask you clearly to provide in this constitution means which will enable the people readily to amend it if at any point it works injustice, and also means which will permit the people themselves by popular vote, after due deliberation and discussion, but finally and without appeal, to settle what the proper construction of any constitutional point is.

It is often said that ours is a government of checks and balances. But this should only mean that these checks and balances obtain as among the several different kinds of representatives of the people—judicial, executive, and legislative—to whom the people have delegated certain portions of their power. It does not mean that the people have parted with their power or cannot resume it. The "division of powers" is merely the division among the representatives of the powers delegated to them; the term must not be held to mean that the people have divided their power with their delegates. The power is the people's, and only the people's. It is right and proper that provision should be made rendering it necessary for the people to take ample time to make up their minds on any point; but there should also be complete provision to have their decision put into immediate and living effect when it has thus been deliberately and definitely reached.

I hold it to be the duty of every public servant, and of every man who in public or private life holds a position of leadership in thought or action, to endeavor honestly and fearlessly to guide his fellow countrymen to right decisions; but I emphatically dissent from the view that it is either wise or necessary to try to devise methods which under the Constitution will automatically prevent the people from deciding for themselves what governmental action they deem just and proper.

It is impossible to invent constitutional devices which will prevent the popular will from being effective for wrong without also preventing it from being effective for right.

The only safe course to follow in this great American democracy is to provide for making the popular judgment really effective. . . .

Lincoln, with his clear vision, his ingrained sense of justice, and his spirit of kindly friendliness to all, forecast our present struggle and saw the way out. What he said should be pondered by capitalist and working man alike. He spoke as follows (I condense):

"I hold that while man exists it is his duty to improve not only his conditions but to assist in ameliorating mankind. Labor is prior to and independent of capital. Labor is the superior of capital, and deserves much the higher consideration. Capital has its rights, which are as worthy of protection as any other rights. Nor should this lead to a war upon property. Property is the fruit of labor. Property is desirable, is a positive good in the world. Let not him who is houseless pull down the house of another, but let him work diligently and build one for himself, thus by example assuring that his own shall be safe from violence when built."

This last sentence characteristically shows Lincoln's homely, kindly common sense. His is the attitude that we ought to take. He showed the proper sense of proportion in his relative estimates of capital and labor, of human rights and the rights of wealth. Above all, in what he thus said, as on so many other occasions, he taught the indispensable lesson of the need of wise kindliness and charity, of sanity and moderation, in the dealings of men one with another.

We should discriminate between two purposes we have in view. The first is the effort to provide what are themselves the ends of good government; the second is the effort to provide proper machinery for the achievement of these ends.

The ends of good government in our democracy are to secure by genuine popular rule a high average of moral and material well-being among our citizens.

It has been well said that in the past we have paid attention only to the accumulation of prosperity, and that from henceforth we must pay equal attention to the proper distinction of prosperity. This is true. The only prosperity worth having is that which affects the mass of the people. We are bound to strive for the fair distribution of prosperity. But it behooves us to remember that there is no use in devising methods for the proper distribution of prosperity unless the prosperity is there to distribute. I hold it to be our duty to see that the wage-worker, the small producer, the ordinary consumer, shall get their fair share of the benefit of business prosperity. But it either is or ought to be evident to every one that business has to prosper before anybody can get any benefit from it. Therefore I hold that he is the real Progressive, that he is the genuine champion of the people, who endeavors to shape the policy alike of the nation and of the several States so as to encourage legitimate and honest business at the same time that he wars against all crookedness and injustice and unfairness and tyranny in the business world (for of course we can only get business put on a basis of permanent prosperity when the element of injustice is taken out of it).

This is the reason why I have for so many years insisted, as regards our National Government, that it is both futile and mischievous to endeavor to correct the evils of big business by an attempt to restore business conditions as they were in the middle of the last century, before railways and telegraphs had rendered larger business organizations both inevitable and desirable. The effort to restore such conditions, and to trust for justice solely to such proposed restoration, is as foolish as if we should attempt to arm our troops with the flintlocks of Washington's Continentals instead of with modern weapons of precision. Flintlock legislation, of the kind that seeks to prohibit all combinations, good or bad, is bound to fail, and the effort, in so far as it accomplishes anything at all, merely means that some of the worst combinations are not checked, and that honest business is checked.

What is needed is, first, the recognition that modern business conditions have come to stay, in so far at least as these conditions mean that business must be done in larger units, and then the cool-headed and resolute determination to introduce an effective method of regulating big corporations so as to help legitimate business as an incident to thoroughly and completely safeguarding the interests of the people as a whole.

We are a business people. The tillers of the soil, the wage-workers, the business men—these are the three big and vitally important divisions of our population. The welfare of each division is vitally necessary to the welfare of the people as a whole. The great mass of business is of course done by men whose business is either small or of moderate size. The middle-sized business men form an element of strength which is of literally incalculable value to the nation. Taken as a class, they are among our best citizens. They have not been seekers after enormous fortunes; they have been moderately and justly prosperous, by reason of dealing fairly with their customers, competitors, and employees. They are satisfied with a legitimate profit that will pay their expenses of living and lay by something for those who come after, and the additional amount necessary for the betterment and improvement of their plant. The average business man of this type is, as a rule, a leading citizen of his community, foremost in everything that tells for its betterment, a man whom his neighbors look up to and respect; he is in no sense dangerous to his community, just because he is an integral part of his community, bone of its bone and flesh of its flesh. His life fibres are intertwined with the life fibres of his fellow citizens. Yet nowadays many men of this kind, when they come to make necessary trade agreements with one another, find themselves in danger of becoming unwitting transgressors of the law, and are at a loss to know what the law forbids and what it permits. This is all wrong. There should be a fixed governmental policy, a policy which shall clearly define and punish wrongdoing, and shall give in advance full information to any man as to just what he can and just what he cannot legally and properly do. It is absurd and wicked to treat the deliberate lawbreaker as on an exact par with the man eager to obey the law, whose only desire is to find out from some competent governmental authority what the law is and then live up to it. It is absurd to endeavor to regulate business in the interest of the public by means of long-drawn lawsuits without any accompaniment of administrative control and regulation, and without any attempt to discriminate between the honest man who has succeeded in business because of rendering a service to the public and the dishonest man who has succeeded in business by cheating the public.

So much for the small business man and the middle-sized business man. Now for big business.

It is imperative to exercise over big business a control and supervision which is unnecessary as regards small business. All business must be conducted under the law, and all business men, big or little, must act justly. But a wicked big interest is necessarily more dangerous to the community than a wicked little interest. "Big business" in the past has been responsible for much of the special privilege which must be unsparingly cut out of our national life. I do not believe in making mere size of and by itself criminal. The mere fact of size, however, does unquestionably carry the potentiality of such grave wrongdoing that there should be by law provision made for the strict supervision and regulation of these great industrial concerns doing an interstate business, much as we now regulate the transportation agencies which are engaged in interstate business. The antitrust law does good in so far as it can be invoked against combinations which really are monopolies or which restrict production or which artificially raise prices. But in so far as its workings are uncertain, or as it threatens corporations which have not been guilty of antisocial conduct, it does harm. Moreover, it cannot by itself accomplish more than a trifling part of the governmental regulation of big business which is needed. The nation and the States must cooperate in this matter.

Among the States that have entered this field Wisconsin has taken a leading place. Following Senator La Follette, a number of practical workers and thinkers in Wisconsin have turned that State into an experimental laboratory of wise governmental action in aid of social and industrial justice. They have initiated the kind of progressive government which means not merely the preservation of true democracy, but the extension of the principle of true democracy into industrialism as well as into politics. One prime reason why the State has been so successful in this policy lies in the fact that it has done justice to corporations precisely as it has exacted justice from them. Its Public Utilities Commission in a recent report answered certain critics as follows:

"To be generous to the people of the State at the expense of justice to the carriers would be a species of official brigandage that ought to hold the perpetrators up to the execration of all honest men. Indeed, we have no idea that the people of Wisconsin have the remotist desire to deprive the railroads of the State of aught that, in equality and good conscience, belongs to them, and if any of them have, their wishes cannot be gratified by this Commission."

This is precisely the attitude we should take toward big business. It is the practical application of the principle of the square deal.

Not only as a matter of justice, but in our own interest, we should scrupulously respect the rights of honest and decent business and should encourage it where its activities make, as they often do make, for the common good. It is for the advantage of all of us when business prospers. It is for the advantage of all of us to have the United States become the leading nation in international trade, and we should not deprive this nation, we should not deprive this people, of the instruments best adapted to secure such international commercial supremacy.

In other words, our demand is that big business give the people a square deal and that the people give a square deal to any man engaged in big business who honestly endeavors to do what is right and proper.

On the other hand, any corporation, big or little, which has gained its position by unfair methods and by interference with the rights of others, which has raised prices or limited output in improper fashion and been guilty of demoralizing and corrupt practices, should not only be broken up, but it should be made the business of some competent governmental body by constant supervision to see that it does not come together again, save under such strict control as to insure the community against all danger of a repetition of the bad conduct. The chief trouble with big business has arisen from the fact that big business has so often refused to abide by the principle of the square deal; the opposition which I personally have encountered from big business has in every case arisen, not because I did not give a square deal, but because I did.

All business into which the element of monopoly in any way or degree enters, and where it proves in practice impossible totally to eliminate this element of monopoly, should be carefully supervised, regulated, and controlled by governmental authority; and such control should be exercised by administrative, rather than by judicial, officers. No effort should be made to destroy a big corporation merely because it is big, merely because it has shown itself a peculiarly efficient business instrument. But we should not fear, if necessary, to bring the regulation of big corporations to the point of controlling conditions so that the wage-worker shall have a wage more than sufficient to cover the bare cost of living, and hours of labor not so excessive as to wreck his strength by the strain of unending toil and leave him unfit to do his duty as a good citizen in the community.

Where regulation by competition (which is, of course, preferable) proves insufficient, we should not shrink from bringing governmental regulation to the point of control of monopoly prices if it should ever become necessary to do so, just as in exceptional cases railway rates are now regulated.

In emphasizing the part of the administrative department in regulating combinations and checking absolute monopoly, I do not, of course, overlook the obvious fact that the legislature and the judiciary must do their part. The legislature should make it more clear exactly what methods are illegal, and then the judiciary will be in a better position to punish adequately and relentlessly those who insist on defying the clear legislative decrees.

I do not believe any absolute private monopoly is justified, but if our great combinations are properly supervised, so that immoral practices are prevented, absolute monopoly will not come to pass, as the laws of competition and efficiency are against it.

The important thing is this: that, under such government recognition as we may give to that which is beneficient and wholesome in large business organizations, we shall be most vigilant never to allow them to crystallize into a condition which shall make private initiative difficult. It is of the utmost importance that in the future we shall keep the broad path of opportunity just as open and easy for our children as it was for our fathers during the period which has been the glory of America's industrial history—that it shall be not only possible but easy for an ambitious man, whose character has so impressed itself upon his neighbors that they are willing to give him capital and credit, to start in business for himself, and, if his superior efficiency deserves it, to triumph over the biggest organization that may happen to exist in his particular field. Whatever practices upon the part of large combinations may threaten to discourage such a man, or deny to him that which in the judgment of the community is a square deal, should be specifically defined by the statutes as crimes. And in every case the individual corporation officer responsible for such unfair dealing should be punished.

We grudge no man a fortune which represents his own power and sagacity exercised with entire regard to the welfare

of his fellows. We have only praise for the business man whose
business success comes as an incident to doing good work for
his fellows. But we should so shape conditions that a fortune
shall be obtained only in honorable fashion, in such fashion
that its gaining represents benefit to the community.

In a word, then, our fundamental purpose must be to secure genuine equality of opportunity. No man should receive
a dollar unless that dollar has been fairly earned. Every
dollar received should represent a dollar's worth of service
rendered. No watering of stocks should be permitted; and it
can be prevented only by close governmental supervision of
all stock issues, so as to prevent overcapitalization.

We stand for the rights of property, but we stand even more
for the rights of man.

We will protect the rights of the wealthy man, but we maintain that he holds his wealth subject to the general right of
the community to regulate its business use as the public welfare requires.

We also maintain that the nation and the several States
have the right to regulate the terms and conditions of labor,
which is the chief element of wealth, directly in the interest
of the common good. It is our prime duty to shape the industrial and social forces so that they may tell for the material
and moral upbuilding of the farmer and the wage-worker, just
as they should do in the case of the business man. You framers
of this constitution be careful so to frame it that under it the
people shall leave themselves free to do whatever is necessary
in order to help the farmers of the State to get for themselves
and their wives and children not only the benefits of better
farming but also those of better business methods and better
conditions of life on the farm.

Moreover, shape your constitutional action so that the people will be able through their legislative bodies, or, failing
that, by direct popular vote, to provide workmen's compensation acts, to regulate the hours of labor for children and for
women, to provide for their safety while at work, and to
prevent overwork or work under unhygienic or unsafe condi-

tions. See to it that no restrictions are placed upon legislative powers that will prevent the enactment of laws under which your people can promote the general welfare, the common good. Thus only will the "general welfare" clause of our Constitution become a vital force for progress.

*. . . we were very heedless and in a hurry
to be great.*

FIRST INAUGURAL ADDRESS

By Woodrow Wilson (1856–1924)

ON MARCH 4, 1913, President Wilson restated in this address the
principles of the "New Freedom" on which he had based his
campaign. It is an eloquent declaration of faith in the United
States and its people, and a ringing call to duty.

MY FELLOW CITIZENS: There has been a change of government. It began two years ago, when the House of Representatives became Democratic by a decisive majority. It has now been completed. The Senate about to assemble will also be Democratic. The offices of President and Vice-President have been put into the hands of Democrats. What does the change mean? That is the question that is uppermost in our minds to-day. That is the question I am going to try to answer, in order, if I may, to interpret the occasion.

It means much more than the mere success of a party. The success of a party means little except when the Nation is using that party for a large and definite purpose. No one can mistake the purpose for which the Nation now seeks to use the Democratic Party. It seeks to use it to interpret a change in its own plans and point of view. Some old things with which we had grown familiar, and which had begun to creep into the very habit of our thought and of our lives, have altered their aspect as we have latterly looked critically upon them, with fresh, awakened eyes; have dropped their disguises and shown themselves alien and sinister. Some new things, as we look frankly upon them, willing to comprehend their real character, have come to assume the aspect of things long believed in and familiar, stuff of our own convictions. We have been refreshed by a new insight into our own life.

We see that in many things that life is very great. It is incomparably great in its material aspects, in its body of wealth, in the diversity and sweep of its energy, in the industries which have been conceived and built up by the genius of individual men and the limitless enterprise of groups of men. It is great, also, very great, in its moral force.

Nowhere else in the world have noble men and women exhibited in more striking forms the beauty and the energy of sympathy and helpfulness and counsel in their efforts to rectify wrong, alleviate suffering, and set the weak in the way of strength and hope. We have built up, moreover, a great system of government, which has stood through a long age as in many respects a model for those who seek to set liberty upon foundations that will endure against fortuitous change, against storm and accident. Our life contains every great thing, and contains it in rich abundance.

But the evil has come with the good, and much fine gold has been corroded. With riches has come inexcusable waste. We have squandered a great part of what we might have used, and have not stopped to conserve the exceeding bounty of nature, without which our genuis for enterprise would have been worthless and impotent, scorning to be careful, shamefully prodigal as well as admirably efficient. We have been proud of our industrial achievements, but we have not hitherto stopped thoughtfully enough to count the human cost, the cost of lives snuffed out, of energies overtaxed and broken, the fearful physical and spiritual cost to the men and women and children upon whom the dead weight and burden of it all has fallen pitilessly the years through. The groans and agony of it all had not yet reached our ears, the solemn, moving undertone of our life, coming up out of the mines and factories and out of every home where the struggle had its intimate and familiar seat. With the great Government went many deep secret things which we too long delayed to look into and scrutinize with candid, fearless eyes. The great Government we loved has too often been made use of for private and selfish purposes, and those who used it had forgotten the people.

At last a vision has been vouchsafed us of our life as a whole. We see the bad with the good, the debased and decadent with the sound and vital. With this vision we approach new affairs. Our duty is to cleanse, to reconsider, to restore, to correct the evil without impairing the good, to purify and humanize every process of our common life without weakening or sentimentalizing it. There has been something crude and heartless and unfeeling in our haste to succeed and be great. Our thought has been "Let every man look out for himself, let every generation look out for itself," while we reared giant machinery which made it impossible that any but those who stood at the levers of control should have a chance to look out for themselves. We had not forgotten our morals. We remembered well enough that we had set up a policy which was meant to serve the humblest as well as the most powerful, with an eye single to the standards of justice and fair play, and remembered it with pride. But we were very heedless and in a hurry to be great.

We have come now to the sober second thought. The scales of heedlessness have fallen from our eyes. We have made up our minds to square every process of our national life again with the standards we so proudly set up at the beginning and have always carried at our hearts. Our work is a work of restoration.

We have itemized with some degree of particularity the things that ought to be altered and here are some of the chief items: A tariff which cuts us off from our proper part in the commerce of the world, violates the just principles of taxation, and makes the Government a facile instrument in the hands of private interests; a banking and currency system based upon the necessity of the Government to sell its bonds fifty years ago and perfectly adapted to concentrating cash and restricting credits; an industrial system which, take it on all its sides, financial as well as administrative, holds capital in leading strings, restricts the liberties and limits the opportunities of labor, and exploits without renewing or conserving the natural resources of the country; a body of agricultural activities never yet given the efficiency of great business undertakings or served as it should be through the instrumentality of science taken directly to the farm, or afforded the facilities of credit best suited to its practical needs; water-courses undeveloped, waste places unreclaimed, forests untended, fast disappearing without plan or prospect of renewal, unregarded waste heaps at every mine. We have studied as perhaps no other nation has the most effective means of production, but we have not studied cost or economy as we should either as organizers of industry, as statesmen, or as individuals.

Nor have we studied and perfected the means by which government may be put at the service of humanity, in safeguarding the health of the Nation, the health of its men and its women and its children, as well as their rights in the struggle for existence. This is no sentimental duty. The firm basis of government is justice, not pity. These are matters of justice. There can be no equality or opportunity, the first essential of justice in the body politic, if men and women and children be not shielded in their lives, their very vitality, from the consequences of great industrial and social processes which they can not alter, control, or singly cope with. Society must see to it that it does not itself crush or weaken or damage its own constituent parts. The first duty of law is to keep sound the society it serves. Sanitary laws, pure food laws, and laws determining conditions of labor which individuals are powerless to determine for themselves are intimate parts of the very business of justice and legal efficiency.

These are some of the things we ought to do, and not leave the others undone, the old-fashioned, never-to-be-neglected, fundamental safeguarding of property and of individual right. This is the high enterprise of the new day: To lift everything that concerns our life as a Nation to the light that shines from the hearthfire of every man's conscience and vision of the right. It is inconceivable that we should do this as partisans; it is inconceivable we should do it in ignorance of the facts as they are or in blind haste. We shall restore, not destroy. We shall deal with our economic system as it is and as it may be modified, not as it might be if we had a clean sheet of paper to write upon; and step by step we shall make it what it should be, in the spirit of those who question their own wisdom and seek counsel and knowledge, not shallow self-satisfaction or the excitement of excursions whither they can not tell. Justice, and only justice, shall always be our motto.

And yet it will be no cool process of mere science. The Nation has been deeply stirred, stirred by a solemn passion, stirred by the knowledge of wrong, of ideals lost, of government too often debauched and made an instrument of evil.

The feelings with which we face this new age of right and opportunity sweep across our heartstrings like some air out of God's own presence, where justice and mercy are reconciled and the judge and the brother are one. We know our task to be no mere task of politics but a task which shall search us through and through, whether we be able to understand our time and the need of our people, whether we be indeed their spokesmen and interpreters, whether we have the pure heart to comprehend and the rectified will to choose our high course of action.

This is not a day of triumph; it is a day of dedication. Here muster, not the forces of party, but the forces of humanity. Men's hearts wait upon us; men's lives hang in the balance; men's hopes call upon us to say what we will do. Who shall live up to the great trust? Who dares fail to try? I summon all honest men, all patriotic, all forward-looking men, to my side. God helping me, I will not fail them, if they will but counsel and sustain me!

. . . the only thing we have to fear is fear itself . . .

FIRST INAUGURAL ADDRESS

By Franklin D. Roosevelt (1882–1945)

THE PASSAGE of the years has taken nothing away from the courage and gallantry of this address, made at a time (March 4, 1933) when more than three years of economic depression had eaten into the national soul.

PRESIDENT HOOVER, Mr. Chief Justice, my friends: This is a day of national consecration, and I am certain that my fellow-Americans expect that on my induction into the Presidency I will address them with a candor and a decision which the present situation of our nation impels.

This is pre-eminently the time to speak the truth, the whole truth, frankly and boldly. Nor need we shrink from honestly facing conditions in our country today. This great nation will endure as it has endured, will revive and will prosper.

So first of all let me assert my firm belief that the only thing we have to fear is fear itself—nameless, unreasoning, unjustified terror which paralyzes needed efforts to convert retreat into advance.

In every dark hour of our national life a leadership of frankness and vigor has met with that understanding and support of the people themselves which is essential to victory. I am convinced that you will again give that support to leadership in these critical days.

In such a spirit on my part and on yours we face our common difficulties. They concern, thank God, only material things. Values have shrunken to fantastic levels; taxes have risen; our ability to pay has fallen, government of all kinds is faced by serious curtailment of income; the means of exchange are frozen in the currents of trade; the withered leaves of industrial enterprise lie on every side; farmers find no markets for their produce; the savings of many years in thousands of families are gone.

More important, a host of unemployed citizens face the grim problem of existence, and an equally great number toil with little return. Only a foolish optimist can deny the dark realities of the moment.

Yet our distress comes from no failure of substance. We are stricken by no plague of locusts. Compared with the perils which our forefathers conquered because they believed and were not afraid, we have still much to be thankful for. Nature still offers her bounty and human efforts have multiplied it. Plenty is at our doorstep, but a generous use of it languishes in the very sight of the supply.

Primarily, this is because the rulers of the exchange of mankind's goods have failed through their own stubbornness and their own incompetence, have admitted their failure and abdicated. Practices of the unscrupulous money changers stand indicted in the court of public opinion, rejected by the hearts and minds of men.

True, they have tried, but their efforts have been cast in the pattern of an outworn tradition. Faced by failure of credit, they have proposed only the lending of more money.

Stripped of the lure of profit by which to induce our people to follow their false leadership, they have resorted to exhortations, pleading tearfully for restored confidence. They know only the rules of a generation of self-seekers.

They have no vision, and when there is no vision the people perish.

The money changers have fled from their high seats in the temple of our civilization. We may now restore that temple to the ancient truths.

The measure of the restoration lies in the extent to which we apply social values more noble than mere monetary profit.

Happiness lies not in the mere possession of money; it lies in the joy of achievement, in the thrill of creative effort.

The joy and moral stimulation of work no longer must be forgotten in the mad chase of evanescent profits. These dark days will be worth all they cost us if they teach us that our true destiny is not to be ministered unto but to minister to ourselves and to our fellow-men.

Recognition of the falsity of material wealth as the standard of success goes hand in hand with the abandonment of the false belief that public office and high political position are to be valued only by the standards of pride of place and personal profit; and there must be an end to a conduct in banking and in business which too often has given to a sacred trust the likeness of callous and selfish wrongdoing.

Small wonder that confidence languishes, for it thrives only on honesty, on honor, on the sacredness of obligations, on faithful protection, on unselfish performance. Without them it cannot live.

Restoration calls, however, not for changes in ethics alone. This nation asks for action, and action now.

Our greatest primary task is to put people to work. This is no unsolvable problem if we face it wisely and courageously.

It can be accomplished in part by direct recruiting by the government itself, treating the task as we would treat the emergency of a war, but at the same time, through this employment, accomplishing greatly needed projects to stimulate and reorganize the use of our natural resources.

Hand in hand with this, we must frankly recognize the overbalance of population in our industrial centers and, by engaging on a national scale in the redistribution, endeavor to provide a better use of the land for those best fitted for the land.

The task can be helped by definite efforts to raise the values of agricultural products and with this the power to purchase the output of our cities.

It can be helped by preventing realistically the tragedy of the growing loss, through foreclosure, of our small homes and our farms.

It can be helped by insistence that the Federal, State and local governments act forthwith on the demand that their cost be drastically reduced.

It can be helped by the unifying of relief activities which today are often scattered, uneconomical and unequal. It can be helped by national planning for and supervision of all forms of transportation and of communications and other utilities which have a definitely public character.

There are many ways in which it can be helped, but it can never be helped merely by talking about it. We must act, and act quickly.

Finally, in our progress toward a resumption of work we require two safeguards against a return of the evils of the old order; there must be a strict supervision of all banking and credits and investments; there must be an end to speculation with other people's money, and there must be provision for an adequate but sound currency.

These are the lines of attack. I shall presently urge upon a new Congress in special session detailed measures for their fulfillment, and I shall seek the immediate assistance of the several States.

Through this program of action we address ourselves to putting our own national house in order and making income balance outgo.

Our international trade relations, though vastly important, are, in point of time and necessity, secondary to the establishment of a sound national economy.

I favor as a practical policy the putting of first things first. I shall spare no effort to restore world trade by international economic readjustment, but the emergency at home cannot wait on that accomplishment.

The basic thought that guides these specific means of national recovery is not narrowly nationalistic.

It is the insistence, as a first consideration, upon the interdependence of the various elements in, and parts of, the United States—a recognition of the old and permanently important manifestation of the American spirt of the pioneer.

It is the way to recovery. It is the immediate way. It is the strongest assurance that the recovery will endure.

In the field of world policy I would dedicate this nation to the policy of the good neighbor—the neighbor who resolutely respects himself and, because he does so, respects the rights of others—the neighbor who respects his obligations and respects the sanctity of his agreements in and with a world of neighbors.

If I read the temper of our people correctly, we now realize as we have never before, our interdependence on each other; that we cannot merely take, but we must give as well; that if we are to go forward we must move as a trained and loyal army willing to sacrifice for the good of a common discipline, because, without such discipline, no progress is made, no leadership becomes effective.

We are, I know, ready and willing to submit our lives and property to such discipline because it makes possible a leadership which aims at a larger good.

This I propose to offer, pledging that the larger purposes will bind upon us all as a sacred obligation with a unity of duty hitherto evoked only in time of armed strife.

With this pledge taken, I assume unhesitatingly the leadership of this great army of our people, dedicated to a disciplined attack upon our common problems.

Action in this image and to this end is feasible under the form of government which we have inherited from our ancestors.

Our Constitution is so simple and practical that it is possible always to meet extraordinary needs by changes in emphasis and arrangement without loss of essential form.

That is why our constitutional system has proved itself the most superbly enduring political mechanism the modern world has produced. It has met every stress of vast expansion of territory, of foreign wars, of bitter internal strife, of world relations.

It is to be hoped that the normal balance of executive and legislative authority may be wholly adequate to meet the unprecedented task before us. But it may be that an unprecedented demand and need for undelayed action may call for temporary departure from that normal balance of public procedure.

I am prepared under my constitutional duty to recommend the measures that a stricken nation in the midst of a stricken world may require.

These measures, or such other measures as the Congress may build out of its experience and wisdom, I shall seek, within my constitutional authority, to bring to speedy adoption.

But in the event that the Congress shall fail to take one of these two courses, and in the event that the national emergency is still critical, I shall not evade the clear course of duty that will then confront me.

I shall ask the Congress for the one remaining instrument to meet the crisis—broad executive power to wage a war against the emergency as great as the power that would be given me if we were in fact invaded by a foreign foe.

For the trust reposed in me I will return the courage and the devotion that befit the time. I can do no less.

We face the arduous days that lie before us in the warm courage of national unity; with the clear consciousness of seeking old and precious moral values; with the clean satisfaction that comes from the stern performance of duty by old and young alike.

We aim at the assurance of a rounded and permanent national life.

We do not distrust the future of essential democracy. The people of the United States have not failed. In their need they have registered a mandate that they want direct, vigorous action.

They have asked for discipline and direction under leadership. They have made me the present instrument of their wishes. In the spirit of the gift I take it.

In this dedication of a nation we humbly ask the blessing of God. May He protect each and every one of us! May He guide me in the days to come!

In war there can be no substitute for victory.

ADDRESS BEFORE CONGRESS

By General of the Army Douglas MacArthur

FOLLOWING his return from the East to the United States, General MacArthur delivered this address on April 19, 1951, before a joint meeting of the Congress.

MR. PRESIDENT, Mr. Speaker, and distinguished members of the Congress: I stand on this rostrum with a sense of deep humility and pride—humility in the wake of those great architects of our history who have stood here before me, pride in the reflection that this home of legislative debate represents human liberty in the purest form yet devised.

Here are centered the hopes and aspirations and faiths of the entire human race.

I do not stand here as advocate of any partisan cause, for the issues are fundamental and reach quite beyond the realm of partisan considerations. They must be resolved on the highest plane of national interest if our course is to prove sound and our future protected.

I trust, therefore, that you will do me the justice of receiving that which I have to say as solely expressing the considered viewpoint of a fellow American.

I address you with neither rancor nor bitterness in the fading twilight of life, with but one purpose in mind: To serve my country.

The issues are global, and so interlocked that to consider the problems of one sector oblivious to those of another is to court disaster for the whole. While Asia is commonly referred to as the gateway to Europe, it is no less true that Europe is the gateway to Asia, and the broad influence of the one can not fail to have its impact upon the other. There are those who claim our strength is inadequate to protect on both fronts, that we cannot divide our effort. I can think of no greater expression of defeatism.

If a potential enemy can divide his strength on two fronts, it is for us to counter his effort. The communist threat is a global one. Its successful advance in one sector threatens the destruction of every other sector. You can not appease or otherwise surrender to communism in Asia without simultaneously undermining our efforts to halt its advance in Europe.

Beyond pointing out these general truisms, I shall confine my discussion to the general areas of Asia.

Before one may objectively assess the situation now existing there he must comprehend something of Asia's past and the revolutionary changes which have marked her course up to the present. Long exploited by the so-called colonial powers, with little opportunity to achieve any degree of social justice, individual dignity, or a higher standard of life such as guided our own noble administration in the Philippines, the people of Asia found their opportunity in the war just past to throw off the shackles of colonialism and now see the dawn of new opportunity, and heretofore unfelt dignity, and self-respect of political freedom.

Mustering half of the earth's population, and 60 per cent of its natural resources, these peoples are rapidly consolidating a new force, both moral and material, with which to raise the living standard and erect adaptation of the design of modern progress to their own distinct cultural environments.

Whether one adheres to the concept of colonialization or not, this is the direction of Asian progress and it may not be stopped. It is a corollary to the shift of the world economic frontiers as the whole epicenter of world affairs rotates toward the area whence it started.

In this situation, it becomes vital that our own country orient its policies in consonance with this basic evolutionary condition rather than pursue a course blind to reality that the colonial era is now past and the Asian peoples covet the right to shape their own free destiny. What they seek now is friendly guidance, understanding and support, not imperious direction, the dignity of equality and not the shame of subjugation.

Their pre-war standard of life, pitifully low, is infinitely lower now in the devastation left in war's wake. World ideologies play little part in Asian thinking and are little understood.

What the people strive for is the opportunity for a little more food in their stomachs, a little better clothing on their backs and a little firmer roof over their heads, and the realization of the normal nationalist urge for political freedom.

These political-social conditions have but an indirect bearing upon our own national security, but do form a backdrop to contemporary planning which must be thoughtfully considered if we are to avoid the pitfalls of unrealism.

Of more direct and immediate bearing upon our national security are the changes wrought in the strategic potential of the Pacific ocean in the course of the past war.

Prior thereto the western strategic frontier of the United States lay on the littoral line of the Americas, with an exposed island salient extending out through Hawaii, Midway and Guam to the Philippines. That salient proved not an outpost of strength but an avenue of weakness along which the enemy could and did attack. The Pacific was a potential area of advance for any predatory force intent upon striking at the bordering land areas.

All this was changed by our Pacific victory. Our strategic frontier then shifted to embrace the entire Pacific ocean, which became a vast moat to protect us as long as we hold it. Indeed, it acts as a protective shield for all of the Americas and all free lands of the Pacific ocean area. We control it to the shores of Asia by a chain of islands extending in an arc from the Aleutians to the Marianas, held by us and our free allies.

From this island chain we can dominate with sea and air power every Asiatic port from Vladivostok to Singapore—with sea and air power, every port, as I said, from Vladivostok to Singapore—and prevent any hostile movement into the Pacific.

Any predatory attack from Asia must be an amphibious effort. No amphibious force can be successful without control of the sea lanes and the air over those lanes in its avenue of advance. With naval and air supremacy and modest ground elements to defend bases, any major attack from continental Asia toward us or our friends in the Pacific would be doomed to failure.

Under such conditions, the Pacific no longer represents menacing avenues of approach for a prospective invader. It assumes, instead, the friendly aspect of a peaceful lake.

Our line of defense is a natural one and can be maintained with a minimum of military effort and expense. It envisions no attack against anyone, nor does it provide the bastions essential for offensive operations, but properly maintained, would be an invincible defense against aggression.

The holding of this littoral defense line in the western Pacific is entirely dependent upon holding all segments thereof, for any major breach of that line by an unfriendly power would render vulnerable to determined attack every other major segment. This is a military estimate as to which I have yet to find a military leader who will take exception.

For that reason, I have strongly recommended in the past, as a matter of military urgency, that under no circumstances must Formosa fall under communist control. Such an eventuality would at once threaten the freedom of the Philippines and the loss of Japan and might well force our western frontier back to the coast of California, Oregon, and Washington.

To understand the changes which now appear upon the Chinese mainland, one must understand the changes in Chinese character and culture over the past 50 years. China up to 50 years ago was completely nonhomogenous, being compartmented into groups divided against each other. The war-making tendency was almost nonexistent as they still followed the tenets of the Confucian ideal of pacifist culture.

At the turn of the century under the regime of Chang Tso-lin efforts toward greater homogeneity produced the start of a nationalist urge. This was further and more successfully developed under the leadership of Chiang Kai-shek, but has been brought to its greatest fruition under the present regime to the point that it has now taken on the character of a united nationalism of increasingly dominant aggressive tendencies.

Through the past 50 years the Chinese people have thus

become militarized in their concepts and in their ideals. They now constitute excellent soldiers, with competent staffs and commanders. This has produced a new and dominant power in Asia, which, for its own purposes, is allied with soviet Russia but which in its own concepts and methods has become aggressively imperialistic with a lust for expansion and increased power normal to this type of imperialism.

There is little of the ideological concept either one way or another in the Chinese make-up. The standard of living is so low and the capital accumulation has been so thoroughly dissipated by war that the masses are desperate and eager to follow any leadership which seems to promise the alleviation of woeful stringencies.

I have from the beginning believed that the Chinese Communists' support of the North Koreans was the dominant one. Their interests are at present parallel with those of the soviet, but I believe that the aggressiveness recently displayed not only in Korea but also in Indo-China and Tibet and pointing potentially toward the south reflects predominantly the same lust for the expansion of power which has animated every would-be conqueror since the beginning of time.

The Japanese people since the war have undergone the greatest reformation recorded in modern history. With a commendable will, eagerness to learn, and marked capacity to understand, they have from the ashes left in war's wake erected in Japan an edifice dedicated to the supremacy of individual liberty and personal dignity, and in the ensuing process there has been created a truly representative government committed to the advance of political morality, freedom of economic enterprise, and social justice.

Politically, economically, and socially Japan is now abreast of many free nations of the earth and will not again fail the universal trust. That it may be counted upon to wield a profoundly beneficial influence over the course of events in Asia is attested by the magnificent manner in which the Japanese people have met the recent challenge of war, unrest, and confusion surrounding them from the outside and checked communism within their own frontiers without the slightest slackening in their forward progress.

I sent all four of our occupation divisions to the Korean battlefront without the slightest qualms as to the effect of the resulting power vacuum upon Japan. The results fully justified my faith.

I know of no nation more serene, more orderly and industrious, nor in which richer hopes can be entertained for future constructive service in the advance of the human race.

Of our former ward in the Philippines we can look forward in confidence that the existing unrest will be corrected and a strong and healthy nation will grow in the longer aftermath of the war's terrible destructiveness. We must be patient and understanding and never fail them, as in our hour of need they did not fail us.

A Christian nation, the Philippines stands as a mighty bulwark of Christianity in the far east, and its capacity for high moral leadership in Asia is unlimited.

On Formosa the government of the republic of China has had the opportunity to refute by action much of the malicious gossip which so undermined the strength of its leadership on the Chinese mainland. The Formosan people are receiving a just and enlightened administration with majority representation in the organs of government, and politically, economically, and socially they appear to be advancing along sound and constructive lines.

With this brief insight into the surrounding areas, I now turn to the Korean conflict.

While I was not consulted prior to the President's decision to intervene in support of the republic of Korea, that decision, from a military standpoint, proved a sound one. As I say, it proved to be a sound one, as we hurled back the invader and decimated his forces. Our victory was complete, and our objective within reach, when Red China intervened with numerically superior ground forces.

This created a new war and an entirely new situation, a situation not contemplated when our forces were committed against the North Korean invaders; a situation which called for new decisions in the diplomatic sphere to permit the realistic adjustment of military strategy. Such decisions have not been forthcoming.

While no man in his right mind would advocate sending our ground forces into continental China, and such was never given thought, the new situation did urgently demand a drastic revision of strategic planning if our political aim was to defeat this new enemy as we had defeated the old one.

Apart from the military need, as I saw it, to neutralize sanctuary protection given the enemy north of the Yalu, I felt that military necessity in the conduct of the war made necessary (1) The intensification of our economic blockade against China; (2) The imposition of a naval blockade against the China coast; (3) Removal of restrictions on air reconnaissance of China's coastal area and of Manchuria; (4) Removal of restrictions on the forces of the republic of China on Formosa, with logistical support to contribute to their effective operations against the common enemy.

For entertaining these views, all professionally designed to support our forces in Korea and to bring hostilities to an end with the least possible delay and at a saving of countless American and allied lives, I have been severely criticized in lay circles, principally abroad, despite my understanding that from a military standpoint the above views have been fully shared in the past by practically every military leader concerned with the Korean campaign, including our own joint chiefs of staff.

I called for reinforcements, but was informed that reinforcements were not available. I made clear that if not permitted to destroy the enemy built-up bases north of the Yalu, if not permitted to utilize the friendly Chinese force of some 600,000 men on Formosa, if not permitted to blockade the China coast to prevent the Chinese Reds from getting succor from without, and if there was to be no hope of major reinforcements, the position of the command from the military standpoint forbade victory.

We could hold in Korea by constant maneuver and in an area where our supply line advantages were in balance with the supply line disadvantages of the enemy, but we could hope at best for only an indecisive campaign with its terrible and constant attrition upon our forces if the enemy utilized its full military potential.

I have constantly called for the new political decisions essential to a solution.

Efforts have been made to distort my position. It has been said in effect that I was a warmonger. Nothing could be further from the truth. I know war as few other men now living know it, and nothing to me is more revolting. I have long advocated its complete abolition, as its very destructiveness on both friend and foe has rendered it useless as a means of settling international disputes.

Indeed, the second day of September, 1945, just following the surrender of the Japanese nation on the battleship *Missouri*, I formally cautioned as follows:

"Men since the beginning of time have sought peace. Various methods through the ages have been attempted to devise an international process to prevent or settle disputes between nations. From the very start workable methods were found in so far as individual citizens were concerned, but the mechanics of an instrumentality of larger international scope have never been successful. Military alliances, balances of power, leagues of nations, all in turn failed, leaving the only path to be by way of the crucible of war. The utter destructiveness of war now blocks out this alternative. We have had our last chance. If we will not devise some greater and more equitable system, our Armageddon will be at our door. The problem basically is theological and involves a spiritual recrudescence and improvement of human character that will synchronize with our almost matchless advances in science, art, literature and all the material and cultural developments of the past 2,000 years. It must be of the spirit if we are to save the flesh."

But once war is forced upon us, there is no other alternative than to apply every available means to bring it to a swift end. War's very object is victory, not prolonged indecision.

In war there can be no substitute for victory.

There are some who for varying reasons would appease Red China. They are blind to history's clear lesson, for history teaches with unmistakable emphasis that appeasement but begets new and bloodier wars. It points to no single instance where this end has justified that means, where appeasement has led to more than a sham peace. Like blackmail, it lays the basis for new and successive greater demands until, as in blackmail, violence becomes the only other alternative. Why, my soldiers asked me, surrender military advantages to an enemy in the field? I could not answer.

Some may say, to avoid spread of the conflict into an all-out war with China. Others, to avoid soviet intervention. Neither explanation seems valid, for China is already engaging with the maximum power it can commit, and the soviet will not necessarily mesh its actions with our moves. Like a cobra, any new enemy will more likely strike whenever it feels that the relativity of military and other potentialities is in its favor on a world-wide basis.

The tragedy of Korea is further heightened by the fact that its military action was confined to its territorial limits. It condemns that nation, which it is our purpose to save, to suffer the devastating impact of full naval and air bombardment while the enemy's sanctuaries are fully protected from such attack and devastation.

Of the nations of the world, Korea alone, up to now, is the sole one which has risked its all against communism. The magnificence of the courage and fortitude of the Korean people defies description. They have chosen to risk death rather than slavery. Their last words to me were: "Don't scuttle the Pacific."

I have just left your fighting sons in Korea. They have done their best there, and I can report to you without reservation that they are splendid in every way.

It was my constant effort to preserve them and end this

savage conflict honorably and with the least loss of time and a minimum sacrifice of life. Its growing bloodshed has caused me the deepest anguish and anxiety. Those gallant men will remain often in my thoughts and in my prayers always.

I am closing my 52 years of military service. When I joined the army, even before the turn of the century, it was the fulfillment of all of my boyish hopes and dreams. The world has turned over many times since I took the oath at West Point, and the hopes and dreams have all since vanished, but I still remember the refrain of one of the most popular barracks ballads of that day which proclaimed most proudly that old soldiers never die; they just fade away. And, like the old soldier of that ballad, I now close my military career and just fade away, an old soldier who tried to do his duty as God gave him the light to see that duty. Good-by.

THE DECLARATION OF INDEPENDENCE
in Congress, July 4, 1776

The unanimous declaration of the Thirteen United States of America

Preamble

WHEN, IN THE COURSE of human events, it becomes necessary for one people to dissolve the political bands which have connected them with another, and to assume among the powers of the earth the separate and equal station to which the laws of nature and of nature's God entitle them, a decent respect to the opinions of mankind requires that they should declare the causes which impel them to the separation.

We hold these truths to be self-evident: That all men are created equal; that they are endowed by their Creator with certain unalienable rights; that among these are life, liberty, and the pursuit of happiness; that, to secure these rights, governments are instituted among men, deriving their just powers from the consent of the governed; that whenever any form of government becomes destructive of these ends, it is the right of the people to alter or to abolish it and to institute new government, laying its foundation on such principles, and organizing its powers in such form, as to them shall seem most likely to effect their safety and happiness. Prudence, indeed, will dictate that governments long established should not be changed for light and transient causes;

and, accordingly, all experience hath shown that mankind are more disposed to suffer while evils are sufferable, than to right themselves by abolishing the forms to which they are accustomed. But when a long train of abuses and usurpations, pursuing invariably the same object, evinces a design to reduce them under absolute despotism, it is their right, it is their duty, to throw off such government and to provide new guards for their future security. Such has been the patient sufferance of these colonies; and such is now the necessity which constrains them to alter their former systems of government.

Specific Charges against the King

The history of the present King of Great Britain is a history of repeated injuries and usurpations, all having in direct object the establishment of an absolute tyranny over these States. To prove this, let facts be submitted to a candid world:

He has refused his assent to laws, the most wholesome and necessary for the public good.

He has forbidden his Governors to pass laws of immediate and pressing importance, unless suspended in their operation till his assent should be obtained; and, when so suspended, he has utterly neglected to attend to them.

He has refused to pass other laws for the accommodation of large districts of people, unless those people would relinquish the right of representation in the Legislature, a right inestimable to them and formidable to tyrants only.

He has called together legislative bodies at places unusual, uncomfortable, and distant from the depository of their public records, for the sole purpose of fatiguing them into compliance with his measures.

He has dissolved representative Houses repeatedly for opposing with manly firmness his invasions on the rights of the people.

He has refused for a long time after such dissolutions to cause others to be elected; whereby the legislative powers, incapable of annihilation, have returned to the people at large for their exercise; the State remaining, in the meantime, exposed to all the dangers of invasions from without and convulsions within.

He has endeavored to prevent the population of these States; for that purpose obstructing the laws for naturalization of foreigners, refusing to pass others to encourage their migration hither, and raising the conditions of new appropriations of lands.

He has obstructed the administration of justice by refusing his assent to laws for establishing judiciary powers.

He has made judges dependent on his will alone for the tenure of their offices and the amount and payment of their salaries.

He has erected a multitude of new offices, and sent hither swarms of officers to harass our people and eat out their substance.

He has kept among us, in times of peace, standing armies, without the consent of our Legislatures.

He has affected to render the military independent of, and superior to, the civil power.

He has combined with others to subject us to a jurisdiction foreign to our Constitution and unacknowledged by our laws, giving his assent to their acts of pretended legislation:

For quartering large bodies of armed troops among us;

For protecting them, by a mock trial, from punishment for any murders which they should commit on the inhabitants of these States;

For cutting off our trade with all parts of the world;

For imposing taxes on us without our consent;

For depriving us, in many cases, of the benefits of trial by jury;

For transporting us beyond seas to be tried for pretended offenses;

For abolishing the free system of English laws in a neighboring province, establishing therein an arbitrary government, and enlarging its boundaries so as to render it at once an example and fit instrument for introducing the same absolute rule into these colonies;

For taking away our charters, abolishing our most valuable laws, and altering fundamentally the forms of our governments;

For suspending our own Legislatures, and declaring themselves invested with power to legislate for us in all cases whatsoever.

He has abdicated government here by declaring us out of his protection and waging war against us.

He has plundered our seas, ravaged our coasts, burnt our towns, and destroyed the lives of our people.

He is at this time transporting large armies of foreign mercenaries to complete the works of death, desolation, and tyranny, already begun with circumstances of cruelty and perfidy scarcely paralleled in the most barbarous ages, and totally unworthy the head of a civilized nation.

He has constrained our fellow citizens, taken captive on the high seas, to bear arms against their country, to become the executioners of their friends and brethren, or to fall themselves by their hands.

He has excited domestic insurrections amongst us, and has endeavored to bring on the inhabitants of our frontiers the merciless Indian savages, whose known rule of warfare is an undistinguished destruction of all ages, sexes, and conditions.

In every stage of these oppressions we have petitioned for redress in the most humble terms: our repeated petitions have been answered only by repeated injury. A prince, whose character is thus marked by every act which may define a tyrant, is unfit to be the ruler of a free people.

Nor have we been wanting in attentions to our British brethren. We have warned them from time to time of attempts by their Legislature to extend an unwarrantable jurisdiction over us. We have reminded them of the circumstances of our emigration and settlement here. We have appealed to their native justice and magnanimity, and we have conjured them by the ties of our common kindred to disavow these usurpations which would inevitably interrupt our connections and correspondence. They, too, have been deaf to the voice of justice and consanguinity. We must, therefore, acquiesce in the necessity which denounces our separation, and hold them, as we hold the rest of mankind, enemies in war; in peace, friends.

Conclusion and Declaration

WE, THEREFORE, the Representatives of the United States of America, in General Congress assembled, appealing to the Supreme Judge of the world for the rectitude of our intentions, do, in the name and by the authority of the good people of these colonies, solemnly publish and declare that these United Colonies are, and of right ought to be, FREE AND INDEPENDENT STATES; that they are absolved from all allegiance to the British Crown, and that all political connection between them and the State of Great Britain is, and ought to be, totally dissolved; and that as free and independent States they have full power to levy war, conclude peace, contract alliances, establish commerce, and to do all other acts and things which independent States may of right do. And for the support of this declaration, with a firm reliance on the protection of Divine Providence, we mutually pledge to each other our lives, our fortunes, and our sacred honor.

JOHN HANCOCK

The Signers

NEW HAMPSHIRE

Josiah Bartlett
Wm. Whipple
Matthew Thornton

MASSACHUSETTS BAY

Saml. Adams
John Adams
Robt. Treat Paine
Elbridge Gerry

RHODE ISLAND

Step. Hopkins
William Ellery

CONNECTICUT

Roger Sherman
Sam'el Huntington
Wm. Williams
Oliver Wolcott

NEW YORK

Wm. Floyd
Phil. Livingston
Frans. Lewis
Lewis Morris

NEW JERSEY

Richd. Stockton
Jno. Witherspoon
Fras. Hopkinson
John Hart
Abra. Clark

PENNSYLVANIA

Robt. Morris
Benjamin Rush
Benja. Franklin
John Morton
Geo. Clymer
Jas. Smith
Geo. Taylor
James Wilson
Geo. Ross

DELAWARE

Caesar Rodney
Geo. Read
Tho. M'Kean

MARYLAND

Samuel Chase
Wm. Paca
Thos. Stone
Charles Carroll of
Carrollton

VIRGINIA

George Wythe
Richard Henry Lee
Th. Jefferson
Benja. Harrison
Thos. Nelson, Jr.
Francis Lightfoot
Lee
Carter Braxton

NORTH CAROLINA

Wm. Hooper
Joseph Hewes
John Penn

SOUTH CAROLINA

Edward Rutledge
Thos. Heyward,
Junr
Thomas Lynch,
Junr
Arthur Middleton

GEORGIA

Button Gwinnett
Lyman Hall
Geo. Walton

THE CONSTITUTION OF THE UNITED STATES OF AMERICA

PREAMBLE

WE THE PEOPLE of the United States in order to form a more perfect union, establish justice, insure domestic tranquillity, provide for the common defense, promote the general welfare, and secure the blessings of liberty to ourselves and our posterity, do ordain and establish this Constitution for the United States of America.

THE LEGISLATIVE DEPARTMENT
Article I

SECTION 1. All legislative powers herein granted shall be vested in a Congress of the United States, which shall consist of a Senate and House of Representatives.

HOW THE HOUSE OF REPRESENTATIVES IS FORMED

SECTION 2. The House of Representatives shall be composed of members chosen every second year by the people of the several States, and the electors in each State shall have the qualifications requisite for electors of the most numerous branch of the State Legislature.

No person shall be a Representative who shall not have attained to the age of twenty-five years, and been seven years a citizen of the United States, and who shall not, when elected, be an inhabitant of that State in which he shall be chosen.

Representatives and direct taxes shall be apportioned

among the several States which may be included within this Union, according to their respective numbers, which shall be determined by adding to the whole number of free persons, including those bound to service for a term of years, and excluding Indians not taxed, three-fifths of all other persons. The actual enumeration shall be made within three years after the first meeting of the Congress of the United States, and within every subsequent term of ten years, in such manner as they shall by law direct. The number of Representatives shall not exceed one for every thirty thousand, but each State shall have at least one Representative; and until such enumeration shall be made, the State of New Hampshire shall be entitled to choose three, Massachusetts eight, Rhode Island and Providence Plantations one, Connecticut five, New York six, New Jersey four, Pennsylvania eight, Delaware one, Maryland six, Virginia ten, North Carolina five, South Carolina five, and Georgia three.

When vacancies happen in the representation from any State, the executive authority thereof shall issue writs of election to fill such vacancies.

The House of Representatives shall choose their Speaker and other officers; and shall have the sole power of impeachment.

HOW THE SENATE IS FORMED

SECTION 3. The Senate of the United States shall be composed of two Senators from each State, chosen by the Legislature thereof, for six years; and each Senator shall have one vote.

Immediately after they shall be assembled in consequence of the first election, they shall be divided as equally as may be into three classes. The seats of the Senators of the first class shall be vacated at the expiration of the second year, of the second class at the expiration of the fourth year, and of the third class at the expiration of the sixth year, so that one-third may be chosen every second year; and if vacancies happen by resignation, or otherwise, during the recess of the Legislature of any State, the Executive thereof may make temporary appointments until the next meeting of the Legislature, which shall then fill such vacancies.

No person shall be a Senator who shall not have attained to the age of thirty years, and been nine years a citizen of the United States, and who shall not, when elected, be an inhabitant of that State for which he shall be chosen.

The Vice President of the United States shall be President of the Senate, but shall have no vote unless they be equally divided.

The Senate shall choose their other officers, and also a president *pro tempore,* in the absence of the Vice President, or when he shall exercise the office of President of the United States.

The Senate shall have the sole power to try all impeachments. When sitting for that purpose, they shall be on oath or affirmation. When the President of the United States is tried, the Chief Justice shall preside, and no person shall be convicted without the concurrence of two-thirds of the members present.

Judgment in cases of impeachment shall not extend further than to removal from office, and disqualification to hold and enjoy any office of honor, trust, or profit under the United States; but the party convicted shall nevertheless be liable and subject to indictment, trial, judgment, and punishment, according to law.

CONGRESSIONAL ELECTIONS:
TIME OF ASSEMBLING

SECTION 4. The times, places, and manner of holding elections for Senators and Representatives shall be prescribed in each State by the Legislature thereof; but the Congress may at any time by law make or alter such regulations, except as to the places of choosing Senators.

The Congress shall assemble at least once in every year, and such meeting shall be on the first Monday in December, unless they shall by law appoint a different day.

RULES AND PROCEDURE OF CONGRESS

SECTION 5. Each House shall be the judge of the elections, returns, and qualifications of its own members, and a majority of each shall constitute a quorum to do business; but a smaller number may adjourn from day to day, and may be authorized to compel the attendance of absent members, in such manner and under such penalties as each House may provide.

Each House may determine the rules of its proceedings, punish its members for disorderly behavior, and, with the concurrence of two-thirds, expel a member.

Each House shall keep a journal of its proceedings, and from time to time publish the same, excepting such parts as may in their judgment require secrecy; and the yeas and nays of the members of either House on any question shall, at the desire of one-fifth of those present, be entered on the journal.

Neither House, during the session of Congress, shall, without the consent of the other, adjourn for more than three days, nor to any other place than that in which the two Houses shall be sitting.

PRIVILEGES AND RESTRICTIONS
OF CONGRESSMEN

SECTION 6. The Senators and Representatives shall receive a compensation for their services, to be ascertained by law and paid out of the Treasury of the United States. They shall in all cases, except treason, felony, and breach of the peace, be privileged from arrest during their attendance at the session of their respective Houses, and in going to and returning from the same; and for any speech or debate in either House they shall not be questioned in any other place.

No Senator or Representative shall, during the time for which he was elected, be appointed to any civil office under the authority of the United States, which shall have been created, or the emoluments whereof shall have been increased during such time; and no person holding any office under the United States shall be a member of either House during his continuance in office.

HOW FEDERAL LAWS ARE MADE

SECTION 7. All bills for raising revenue shall originate in the House of Representatives; but the Senate may propose or concur with amendments as on other bills.

Every bill which shall have passed the House of Representatives and the Senate shall, before it become a law, be presented to the President of the United States; if he approve he shall sign it, but if not he shall return it with his objections to that House in which it shall have originated, who shall enter the objections at large on their journal and proceed to reconsider it. If after such reconsideration two-thirds of that House shall agree to pass the bill, it shall be sent, together with the objections, to the other House, by which it shall likewise be reconsidered, and if approved by two-thirds of that House, it shall become a law. But in all such cases the votes of both Houses shall be determined by yeas and nays, and the names of the persons voting for and against the bill shall be entered on the journal of each House respectively. If any bill shall not be returned by the President within ten days (Sundays excepted) after it shall have been presented to him, the same shall be a law, in like manner as if he had signed it, unless the Congress by their adjournment prevent its return, in which case it shall not be a law.

Every order, resolution, or vote to which the concurrence of the Senate and House of Representatives may be necessary (except on a question of adjournment) shall be presented to the President of the United States; and before the same shall take effect, shall be approved by him, or being disapproved by him shall be repassed by two-thirds of the Senate and House of Representatives, according to the rules and limitations prescribed in the case of a bill.

POWERS GRANTED TO CONGRESS

SECTION 8. The Congress shall have power to lay and collect taxes, duties, imposts and excises, to pay the debts and provide for the common defense and general welfare of the United States; but all duties, imposts and excises shall be uniform throughout the United States;

To borrow money on the credit of the United States;

To regulate commerce with foreign nations, and among the several States, and with the Indian tribes;

To establish an uniform rule of naturalization, and uniform laws on the subject of bankruptcies throughout the United States;

To coin money, regulate the value thereof and of foreign coin, and fix the standard of weights and measures;

To provide for the punishment of counterfeiting the securities and current coin of the United States;

To establish post offices and post roads;

To promote the progress of science and useful arts, by securing for limited times to authors and inventors the exclusive right to their respective writings and discoveries;

To constitute tribunals inferior to the Supreme Court;

To define and punish piracies and felonies committed on the high seas, and offenses against the law of nations;

To declare war, grant letters of marque and reprisal, and make rules concerning captures on land and water;

To raise and support armies, but no appropriation of money to that use shall be for a longer term than two years;

To provide and maintain a navy;

To make rules for the government and regulation of the land and naval forces;

To provide for calling forth the militia to execute the laws of the Union, suppress insurrections and repel invasions;

To provide for organizing, arming, and disciplining the militia, and for governing such part of them as may be employed in the service of the United States, reserving to the States respectively, the appointment of the officers, and the authority of training the militia according to the discipline prescribed by Congress;

To exercise exclusive legislation, in all cases whatsoever, over such district (not exceeding ten miles square) as may, by cession of particular States, and the acceptance of Congress, become the seat of the government of the United States; and to exercise like authority over all places purchased by the consent of the Legislature of the State in which the same shall be, for the erection of forts, magazines, arsenals, dockyards, and other needful buildings;—and

To make all laws which shall be necessary and proper for carrying into execution the foregoing powers, and all other powers vested by this Constitution in the government of the United States, or in any department or officer thereof.

POWERS DENIED TO
FEDERAL GOVERNMENT

SECTION 9. The migration or importation of such persons as any of the States now existing shall think proper to admit, shall not be prohibited by the Congress prior to the year one thousand eight hundred and eight, but a tax or duty may be imposed on such importation, not exceeding ten dollars for each person.

The privilege of the writ of *habeas corpus* shall not be suspended, unless when in cases of rebellion or invasion the public safety may require it.

No bill of attainder or *ex post facto* law shall be passed.

No capitation or other direct tax shall be laid, unless in proportion to the census or enumeration hereinbefore directed to be taken.

No tax or duty shall be laid on articles exported from any State.

No preference shall be given by any regulation of commerce or revenue to the ports of one State over those of another; nor shall vessels, bound to or from one State, be obliged to enter, clear, or pay duties in another.

No money shall be drawn from the Treasury, but in consequence of appropriations made by laws; and a regular statement and account of the receipts and expenditures of all public money shall be published from time to time.

No title of nobility shall be granted by the United States; and no person holding any office of profit or trust under them shall, without the consent of the Congress, accept of any present, emolument, office, or title, of any kind whatever, from any king, prince, or foreign state.

POWERS DENIED TO STATE GOVERNMENTS

SECTION 10. No State shall enter into any treaty, alliance, or confederation; grant letters of marque and reprisal; coin money; emit bills of credit; make anything but gold and silver coin a tender in payment of debts; pass any bill of attainder, *ex post facto* law, or law impairing the obligation of contracts, or grant any title of nobility.

No State shall, without the consent of the Congress, lay any imposts or duties on imports or exports, except what may be absolutely necessary for executing its inspection laws; and the net produce of all duties and imposts, laid by any State on imports or exports, shall be for the use of the Treasury of the United States; and all such laws shall be subject to the revision and control of the Congress.

No State shall, without the consent of Congress, lay any duty of tonnage, keep troops, or ships of war in time of peace, enter into any agreement or compact with another State, or with a foreign power, or engage in war, unless actually invaded, or in such imminent danger as will not admit of delay.

THE EXECUTIVE DEPARTMENT
Article II

THE PRESIDENT AND VICE PRESIDENT

SECTION 1. The executive power shall be vested in a President of the United States of America. He shall hold his office during the term of four years, and together with the Vice President, chosen for the same term, be elected as follows:

THE ELECTORAL COLLEGE

EACH STATE shall appoint, in such manner as the Legislature thereof may direct, a number of Electors equal to the whole number of Senators and Representatives to which the State may be entitled in the Congress; but no Senator or Representative, or person holding an office of trust or profit under the United States, shall be appointed an Elector.

The Electors shall meet in their respective States, and vote by ballot for two persons, of whom one at least shall not be an inhabitant of the same State with themselves. And they shall make a list of all the persons voted for, and of the number of votes for each; which list they shall sign and certify, and transmit sealed to the seat of the government of the United States, directed to the President of the Senate. The President of the Senate shall, in the presence of the Senate and House of Representatives, open all the certificates, and the votes shall then be counted. The person having the greatest number of votes shall be the President, if such number be a majority of the whole number of Electors appointed; and if there be more than one who have such majority, and have an equal number of votes, then the House of Representatives shall immediately choose by ballot one of them for President; and if no person have a majority, then from the five highest on the list the said House shall in like manner choose the President. But in choosing the President, the votes shall be taken by States, the representation from each

State having one vote; quorum for this purpose shall consist of a member or members from two-thirds of the States, and a majority of all the States shall be necessary to a choice. In every case, after the choice of the President, the person having the greatest number of votes of the Electors shall be the Vice President. But if there should remain two or more who have equal votes, the Senate shall choose from them by ballot the Vice President.

The Congress may determine the time of choosing the Electors, and the day on which they shall give their votes; which day shall be the same throughout the United States.

QUALIFICATIONS,
SUCCESSION BY VICE PRESIDENT, SALARY,
AND OATH OF THE PRESIDENT

No PERSON except a natural-born citizen, or a citizen of the United States at the time of the adoption of this Constitution, shall be eligible to the office of president; neither shall any person be eligible to that office who shall not have attained to the age of thirty-five years, and been fourteen years a resident within the United States.

In case of the removal of the President from office, or of his death, resignation, or inability to discharge the powers and duties of the said office, the same shall devolve on the Vice President, and the Congress may by law provide for the case of removal, death, resignation, or inability, both of the President and Vice President, declaring what officer shall then act as President, and such officer shall act accordingly, until the disability be removed or a President shall be elected.

The President shall, at stated times, receive for his services a compensation, which shall neither be increased nor diminished during the period for which he shall have been elected, and he shall not receive within that period any other emolument from the United States, or any of them.

Before he enter on the execution of his office, he shall

take the following oath or affirmation: "I do solemnly swear (or affirm) that I will faithfully execute the office of President of the United States, and will, to the best of my ability, preserve, protect, and defend the Constitution of the United States."

MILITARY AND PARDONING POWERS
OF THE PRESIDENT

SECTION 2. The President shall be commander in chief of the army and navy of the United States, and of the militia of the several States when called into the actual service of the United States; he may require the opinion, in writing, of the principal officer in each of the executive departments, upon any subject relating to the duties of their respective offices, and he shall have power to grant reprieves and pardons for offenses against the United States, except in cases of impeachment.

TREATIES AND APPOINTMENTS
BY PRESIDENT AND SENATE

HE SHALL have power, by and with the advice and consent of the Senate, to make treaties, provided two-thirds of the Senators present concur; and he shall nominate, and, by and with the advice and consent of the Senate, shall appoint ambassadors, other public ministers and consuls, judges of the Supreme Court, and all other officers of the United States whose appointments are not herein otherwise provided for, and which shall be established by law; but the Congress may by law vest the appointment of such inferior officers, as they think proper, in the President alone, in the courts of law, or in the heads of departments.

The President shall have power to fill up all vacancies that may happen during the recess of the Senate, by granting commissions which shall expire at the end of their next session.

THE EXECUTIVE AND OTHER DUTIES
OF THE PRESIDENT

SECTION 3. He shall from time to time give to the Congress information of the state of the Union, and recommend to their consideration such measures as he shall judge necessary and expedient; he may, on extraordinary occasions, convene both Houses, or either of them, and in case of disagreement between them, with respect to the time of adjournment, he may adjourn them to such time as he shall think proper; he shall receive ambassadors and other public ministers; he shall take care that the laws be faithfully executed, and shall commission all the officers of the United States.

REMOVAL OF EXECUTIVE OFFICERS
FROM OFFICE

SECTION 4. The President, Vice President, and all civil officers of the United States shall be removed from office on impeachment for, and conviction of, treason, bribery, or other high crimes and misdemeanors.

THE JUDICIAL DEPARTMENT
Article III

THE FEDERAL COURTS;
THE TENURE AND SALARY OF JUDGES

SECTION 1. The judicial power of the United States shall be vested in one Supreme Court, and in such inferior courts as the Congress may from time to time ordain and establish. The judges, both of the Supreme and inferior courts, shall hold their offices during good behavior, and shall, at stated times, receive for their services a compensation, which shall not be diminished during their continuance in office.

JURISDICTION OF FEDERAL COURTS
IN GENERAL

SECTION 2. The judicial power shall extend to all cases in law and equity arising under this Constitution, the laws of the United States, and treaties made, or which shall be made, under their authority; to all cases affecting ambassadors, other public ministers and consuls; to all cases of admiralty and maritime jurisdiction; to controversies to which the United States shall be a party; to controversies between two or more States; between a State and citizens of another State; between citizens of different States; between citizens of the same State claiming lands under grants of different States, and between a State, or the citizens thereof, and foreign states, citizens or subjects.

JURISDICTION OF SUPREME COURT

In all cases affecting ambassadors, other public ministers and consuls, and those in which a State shall be party, the Supreme Court shall have original jurisdiction. In all the other cases before mentioned, the Supreme Court shall have appellate jurisdiction, both as to law and fact, with such exceptions and under such regulations as the Congress shall make.

TRIAL BY JURY

The trial of all crimes, except in cases of impeachment, shall be by jury; and such trial shall be held in the State where the said crimes shall have been committed; but when not committed within any State, the trial shall be at such place or places as the Congress may by law have directed.

TREASON:
ITS DEFINITION AND PUNISHMENT

SECTION 3. Treason against the United States shall consist only in levying war against them, or in adhering to their enemies, giving them aid and comfort. No person shall be convicted of treason unless on the testimony of two witnesses to the same overt act, or on confession in open court.

The Congress shall have power to declare the punishment of treason, but no attainder of treason shall work corruption of blood, or forfeiture except during the life of the person attainted.

RELATIONSHIP BETWEEN FEDERAL AND STATE GOVERNMENTS
Article IV

FAITH AND CREDIT BETWEEN STATES

SECTION 1. Full faith and credit shall be given in each State to the public acts, records, and judicial proceedings of every other State. And the Congress may by general laws prescribe the manner in which such acts, records, and proceedings shall be proved, and the effect thereof.

INTERSTATE COMITY REGARDING
CITIZENS AND OTHER PERSONS

SECTION 2. The citizens of each State shall be entitled to all privileges and immunities of citizens in the several States.

A person charged in any State with treason, felony, or other crime, who shall flee from justice and be found in another State, shall, on demand of the executive authority of the State from which he fled, be delivered up, to be removed to the State having jurisdiction of the crime.

No person held to service or labor in one State, under the laws thereof, escaping into another, shall, in consequence of any law or regulation therein, be discharged from such service or labor, but shall be delivered up on claim of the party to whom such service or labor may be due.

ADMISSION OF NEW STATES
TO THE UNION

SECTION 3. New States may be admitted by the Congress into this Union; but no new State shall be formed or erected within the jurisdiction of any other State; nor any State be formed by the junction of two or more States, or parts of States, without the consent of the Legislatures of the States concerned as well as of the Congress.

CONGRESS MAKES RULES RESPECTING GOVERNMENT PROPERTY

THE CONGRESS shall have power to dispose ot and make all needful rules and regulations respecting the territory or other property belonging to the United States; and nothing in this Constitution shall be so construed as to prejudice any claims of the United States or of any particular State.

FEDERAL PROTECTION TO STATES

SECTION 4. The United States shall guarantee to every State in this Union a republican form of government, and shall protect each of them against invasion; and on application of the Legislature, or of the Executive (when the Legislature cannot be convened), against domestic violence.

PROVISIONS FOR AMENDMENTS
Article V

THE CONGRESS, whenever two-thirds of both Houses shall deem it necessary, shall propose amendments to this Constitution, or, on the application of the Legislatures of two-thirds of the several States, shall call a convention for proposing amendments, which, in either case, shall be valid to all intents and purposes, as part of this Constitution, when ratified by the Legislatures of three-fourths of the several States, or by conventions in three-fourths thereof, as the one or the other mode of ratification may be proposed by the Congress; provided that no amendment which may be made prior to the year one thousand eight hundred and eight shall in any manner affect the first and fourth clauses in the ninth section of the first article; and that no State, without its consent, shall be deprived of its equal suffrage in the Senate.

THE CONSTITUTION,
THE SUPREME LAW OF THE LAND
Article VI

PRIOR DEBTS

ALL DEBTS contracted and engagements entered into, before the adoption of this Constitution, shall be as valid against the United States under this Constitution as under the Confederation.

THE SUPREME LAW OF THE LAND
AND THE OBLIGATION OF STATE JUDGES

THIS CONSTITUTION, and the laws of the United States which shall be made in pursuance thereof; and all treaties made, or which shall be made, under the authority of the United States, shall be the supreme law of the land; and the judges in every State shall be bound thereby, anything in the Constitution or laws of any State to the contrary notwithstanding.

FEDERAL AND STATE OFFICERS BOUND BY OATH
TO SUPPORT THE CONSTITUTION

THE SENATORS and Representatives before mentioned, and the members of the several State Legislatures, and all executive and judicial officers, both of the United States and of the several States, shall be bound by oath or affirmation to support this Constitution; but no religious test shall ever be required as a qualification to any office or public trust under the United States.

PROVISIONS FOR RATIFICATION
BY STATES
Article VII

THE RATIFICATION of the conventions of nine states shall be sufficient for the establishment of this Constitution between the States so ratifying the same.

Done in convention by the unanimous consent of the States present, the seventeenth day of September in the year of our Lord one thousand seven hundred and eighty seven, and of the independence of the United States of America the twelfth. In witness whereof we have hereunto subscribed our names.

Attest:
William Jackson,
Secretary

Geo: Washington,
Presidt. and Deputy from Virginia

DELAWARE

Geo: Read
Gunning Bedford, Jun
John Dickinson
Richard Bassett
Jaco: Broom

MARYLAND

James McHenry
Dan of St. Thos. Jenifer
Danl. Carroll

VIRGINIA

John Blair
James Madison, Jr.

NORTH CAROLINA

Wm. Blount
Richd. Dobbs Spaight
Hu Williamson

SOUTH CAROLINA

J. Rutledge
Charles Cotesworth Pinckney
Charles Pinckney
Pierce Butler

NEW HAMPSHIRE

John Langdon
Nicholas Gilman

MASSACHUSETTS

Nathaniel Gorham
Rufus King

CONNECTICUT

Wm. Saml. Johnson
Roger Sherman

NEW YORK

Alexander Hamilton

NEW JERSEY

Wil: Livingston
David Brearley
Wm. Paterson
Jona: Dayton

PENNSYLVANIA

B. Franklin
Thomas Mifflin
Robt. Morris
Geo. Clymer
Thos. FitzSimons
Jared Ingersoll
James Wilson
Gouv Morris

GEORGIA

William Few
Abr Baldwin

THE AMENDMENTS
TO THE CONSTITUTION

THE FIRST TEN amendments to the Constitution, known as "A Bill of Rights," were adopted by the first Congress, called to meet in New York City, March 4, 1789. They were later ratified by the various States, and on December 15, 1791, were made a part of the Constitution.

Amendment I

FREEDOM OF RELIGION, SPEECH, AND THE PRESS; RIGHT OF ASSEMBLY AND PETITION

CONGRESS shall make no law respecting an establishment of religion, or prohibiting the free exercise thereof; or abridging the freedom of speech, or of the press, or the right of the people peaceably to assemble, and to petition the government for a redress of grievances.

Amendment II

RIGHT TO KEEP AND BEAR ARMS

A WELL-REGULATED militia being necessary to the security of a free state, the right of the people to keep and bear arms shall not be infringed.

Amendment III

QUARTERING OF SOLDIERS

No SOLDIER shall in time of peace be quartered in any

house without the consent of the owner, nor in time of war, but in a manner to be prescribed by law.

Amendment IV

REGULATION OF RIGHT OF SEARCH
AND SEIZURE

THE RIGHT of the people to be secure in their persons, houses, papers, and effects, against unreasonable searches and seizures, shall not be violated, and no warrants shall issue but upon probable cause, supported by oath or affirmation, and particularly describing the place to be searched and the persons or things to be seized.

Amendment V

PROTECTION FOR PERSONS
AND THEIR PROPERTY

NO PERSON shall be held to answer for a capital or otherwise infamous crime, unless on a presentment or indictment of a grand jury, except in cases arising in the land or naval forces, or in the militia, when in actual service in time of war or public danger; nor shall any person be subject for the same offense to be twice put in jeopardy of life or limb; nor shall be compelled in any criminal case to be a witness against himself, nor be deprived of life, liberty, or property, without due process of law; nor shall private property be taken for public use, without just compensation.

Amendment VI

RIGHTS OF PERSONS ACCUSED OF CRIME

IN ALL criminal prosecution, the accused shall enjoy the right to a speedy and public trial by an impartial jury of the State and district wherein the crime shall have been committed, which district shall have been previously ascertained by law, and to be informed of the nature and cause of the accusation; to be confronted with the witnesses against him; to have compulsory process for obtaining witnesses in his favor, and to have the assistance of counsel for his defense.

Amendment VII

RIGHT OF TRIAL BY JURY
IN SUITS AT COMMON LAW

IN SUITS at common law, where the value in controversy shall exceed twenty dollars, the right of trial by jury shall be preserved, and no fact tried by a jury shall be otherwise re-examined in any court of the United States, than according to the rules of the common law.

Amendment VIII

PROTECTION AGAINST EXCESSIVE BAIL
AND PUNISHMENTS

EXCESSIVE BAIL shall not be required, nor excessive fines imposed, nor cruel and unusual punishments inflicted.

Amendment IX

CONSTITUTION DOES NOT LIST
ALL INDIVIDUAL RIGHTS

THE ENUMERATION in the Constitution of certain rights shall not be construed to deny or disparage others retained by the people.

Amendment X

POWERS RESERVED TO THE STATES
AND THE PEOPLE

THE POWERS not delegated to the United States by the Constitution, nor prohibited by it to the States, are reserved to the States respectively, or to the people.

Amendment XI

LIMITATION OF POWER OF FEDERAL COURTS

The eleventh amendment, adopted by the third Congress, held in Philadelphia, 1794, was ratified by three-fourths of the States, and made a part of the Constitution, January 8, 1798.

THE JUDICIAL power of the United States shall not be construed to extend to any suit in law or equity, commenced or prosecuted against one of the United States by citizens of another State, or by citizens or subjects of any foreign state.

Amendment XII

REGULATION OF ELECTORAL COLLEGE

The twelfth amendment, adopted by the eighth Congress, held in Washington, D. C., 1803, was ratified by three-fourths of the States, and made a part of the Constitution, September 25, 1804. This amendment was proposed to replace paragraph 3, Section 1, Article II, of the original Constitution.

The Electors shall meet in their respective States and vote by ballot for President and Vice President, one of whom, at least, shall not be an inhabitant of the same State with themselves; they shall name in their ballots the person voted for as President, and in distinct ballots the person voted for as Vice President, and they shall make distinct lists of all persons voted for as President, and of all persons voted for as Vice President, and of the number of votes for each, which lists they shall sign and certify, and transmit sealed to the seat of the government of the United States, directed to the President of the Senate. The President of the Senate shall, in the presence of the Senate and House of Representatives, open all the certificates, and the votes shall then be counted. The person having the greatest number of votes for President shall be the President, if such number be a majority of the whole number of Electors appointed; and if no person have such majority, then from the persons having the highest numbers not exceeding three on the list of those voted for as President, the House of Representatives shall choose immediately, by ballot, the President. But in choosing the President the votes shall be taken by States, the representation from each State having one vote; a quorum for this purpose shall consist of a member or members from two-thirds of the States, and a majority of all the States shall be necessary to a choice. And if the House of Representatives shall not choose a President, whenever the right of choice shall devolve upon them, before the fourth day of March next following, then the Vice President shall act as President, as in the case of the death or other constitutional disability of the President. The person having the greatest number of votes as Vice President shall be the Vice President, if such number be a majority of the whole number of Electors appointed; and if no person have a majority, then from the two highest numbers on the list the Senate shall choose the Vice President; a quorum for the purpose shall consist of two-thirds of the whole number of Senators, and a majority of the whole number shall be necessary to a choice. But no person constitutionally ineligible to the office of President shall be eligible to that of Vice President of the United States.

Amendment XIII

ABOLITION OF SLAVERY

The thirteenth amendment, adopted by the thirty-eigth Congress, held in 1865, was ratified by twenty-seven of the thirty-six States, and made a part of the Constitution, December 18, 1865.

SECTION 1. Neither slavery nor involuntary servitude, except as a punishment for crime whereof the party shall have been duly convicted, shall exist within the United States, or any place subject to their jurisdiction.

SECTION 2. Congress shall have power to enforce this article by appropriate legislation.

Amendment XIV

GUARANTEE OF PROTECTION
TO ALL CITIZENS

The fourteenth amendment, adopted by the thirty-ninth Congress, held in 1866, was ratified by more than three-fourths of the States, and made a part of the Constitution, July 28, 1868.

SECTION 1. All persons born or naturalized in the United States, and subject to the jurisdiction thereof, are citizens of the United States and of the State wherein they reside. No State shall make or enforce any law which shall abridge the privileges or immunities of citizens of the United States; nor shall any State deprive any person of life, liberty, or property, without due process of law; nor deny to any person within its jurisdiction the equal protection of the laws.

APPORTIONMENT OF REPRESENTATIVES

SECTION 2. Representatives shall be apportioned among the several States according to their respective numbers, counting the whole number of persons in each State, excluding Indians not taxed. But when the right to vote at any election for the choice of Electors for President and Vice President of the United States, Representatives in Congress, the executive and judicial officers of a State, or the members of the Legislature thereof, is denied to any of the male inhabitants of such State, being twenty-one years of age, and citizens of the United States, or in any way abridged, except for participation in rebellion, or other crime, the basis of representation therein shall be reduced in the proportion which the number of such male citizens shall bear to the whole number of male citizens twenty-one years of age in such State.

DENIAL OF RIGHTS TO HOLD
PUBLIC OFFICE

SECTION 3. No person shall be a Senator or Representative in Congress, or Elector of President and Vice President, or hold any office, civil or military, under the United States, or under any State, who, having previously taken an oath, as a member of Congress, or as an officer of the United States, or as a member of any State Legislature, or as an executive or judicial officer of any State, to support the Constitution of the United States, shall have engaged in insurrection or rebellion against the same, or given aid or comfort to the enemies thereof. But Congress may, by a vote of two-thirds of each House, remove such disability.

PUBLIC DEBTS

SECTION 4. The validity of the public debt of the United States, authorized by law, including debts incurred for payment of pensions and bounties for services in suppressing insurrection or rebellion, shall not be questioned. But neither the United States nor any State shall assume or pay any debt or obligation incurred in aid of insurrection or rebellion against the United States, or any claim for the loss or emancipation of any slave; but all such debts, obligations, and claims shall be held illegal and void.

SECTION 5. The Congress shall have power to enforce, by appropriate legislation, the provisions of this article.

Amendment XV

SUFFRAGE NOT DENIED BECAUSE OF
RACE, COLOR, OR SERVITUDE

The fifteenth amendment, adopted by the fortieth Congress, held in 1869, was ratified by twenty-nine of the thirty-seven States then in the Union, and made a part of the Constitution, March 30, 1870.

SECTION 1. The right of citizens of the United States to vote shall not be denied or abridged by the United States or by any State on account of race, color, or previous condition of servitude.

SECTION 2. The Congress shall have power to enforce this article by appropriate legislation.

Amendment XVI

POWER TO LEVY INCOME TAXES

The sixteenth amendment, adopted by the sixty-first Congress, held in 1909, was ratified by thirty-eight of the forty-eight States, and made a part of the Constitution, February 25, 1913.

THE CONGRESS shall have power to lay and collect taxes on incomes, from whatever source derived, without apportionment among the several States. and without regard to any census or enumeration.

Amendment XVII

ELECTION OF SENATORS BY DIRECT VOTE

The seventeenth amendment, adopted by the sixty-second Congress, held in 1912, was ratified by thirty-six States, and made a part of the Constitution, May 31, 1913. This amendment was proposed to replace paragraphs 1 and 2, Section 3, Article I.

THE SENATE of the United States shall be composed of two Senators from each State, elected by the people thereof, for six years; and each Senator shall have one vote. The electors in each State shall have the qualifications requisite for electors of the most numerous branch of the State Legislatures.

When vacancies happen in the representation of any State in the Senate, the executive authority of such State shall issue writs of election to fill such vacancies: *Provided,* That the Legislature of any State may empower the Executive thereof to make temporary appointments until the people fill the vacancies by election as the Legislature may direct.

This amendment shall not be so construed as to affect the election or term of any Senator chosen before it becomes valid as part of the Constitution.

Amendment XVIII

PROHIBITION OF MANUFACTURE
AND SALE OF LIQUOR

The eighteenth amendment, adopted by the sixty-fifth Congress, held in 1917, was ratified by three-fourths of the States, and made a part of the Constitution, January 29, 1919.

SECTION 1. After one year from the ratification of this article the manufacture, sale, or transportation of intoxicating liquors within, the importation thereof into, or the exportation thereof from the United States and all territory subject to the jurisdiction thereof for beverage purposes is hereby prohibited.

SECTION 2. The Congress and the several States shall have concurrent power to enforce this article by appropriate legislation.

SECTION 3. This article shall be inoperative unless it shall have been ratified as an amendment to the Constitution by the Legislatures of the several States, as provided in the Constitution, within seven years from the date of the submission hereof to the States by the Congress.

Amendment XIX

SUFFRAGE RIGHTS GRANTED TO WOMEN

The nineteenth amendment, adopted by the sixty-sixth Congress, held in 1919, was ratified by three-fourths of the whole number of States, and made a part of the Constitution, August 26, 1920.

The right of the citizens of the United States to vote shall not be denied or abridged by the United States or by any State on account of sex.

Congress shall have power to enforce this article by appropriate legislation.

Amendment XX

TERMS OF OFFICE OF PRESIDENT, VICE PRESIDENT; TIME CONGRESS SHALL ASSEMBLE

The twentieth amendment, adopted by the seventy-second Congress, held in 1932, was ratified by thirty-nine States, and made a part of the Constitution, February 6, 1933.

SECTION 1. The terms of the President and Vice President shall end at noon on the 20th day of January, and the terms of Senators and Representatives at noon on the 3rd day of January, of the years in which such terms would have ended if this article had not been ratified; and the terms of their successors shall then begin.

SECTION 2. The Congress shall assemble at least once in every year, and such meeting shall begin at noon on the 3d day of January, unless they shall by law appoint a different day.

SECTION 3. If, at the time fixed for the beginning of the term of the President, the President elect shall have died, the Vice President elect shall become President. If a President shall not have been chosen before the time fixed for the beginning of his term, or if the President elect shall have failed to qualify, then the Vice President elect shall act as President until a President shall have qualified; and the Congress may by law provide for the case wherein neither a President elect nor a Vice President elect shall have qualified, declaring who shall then act as President, or the manner in which one who is to act shall be selected, and such person shall act accordingly until a President or Vice President shall have qualified.

SECTION 4. The Congress may by law provide for the case of the death of any of the persons from whom the House of Representatives may choose a President, whenever the right of choice shall have devolved upon them, and for the case of the death of any of the persons from whom the Senate may choose a Vice President whenever the right of choice shall have devolved upon them.

SECTION 5. Sections 1 and 2 shall take effect on the 15th day of October following the ratification of this article.

SECTION 6. This article shall be inoperative unless it shall have been ratified as an amendment to the Constitution by the Legislatures of three-fourths of the several States within seven years from the date of its submission.

Amendment XXI

REPEAL OF PROHIBITION

The twenty-first amendment, adopted by the seventy-second Congress, held in 1933, was ratified by thirty-six States, and made a part of the Constitution, December 5, 1933.

SECTION 1. The eighteenth article of amendment to the Constitution of the United States is hereby repealed.

SECTION 2. The transportation or importation into any State, Territory, or possession of the United States for delivery or use therein of intoxicating liquors, in violation of the laws thereof, is hereby prohibited.

SECTION 3. This article shall be inoperative unless it shall have been ratified as an amendment to the Constitution by conventions in the several States, as provided in the Constitution, within seven years from the date of the submission hereof to the States by the Congress.

Amendment XXII

LIMITING PRESIDENTIAL TERMS
OF OFFICE

The twenty-second amendment was adopted by the eightieth Congress in 1947. On February 26, 1951, Nevada became the thirty-sixth State to ratify it, and the amendment became a part of the Constitution.

No person shall be elected to the office of the President more than twice, and no person who has held the office of President, or acted as President, for more than two years of a term to which some other person was elected President shall be elected to the office of the President more than once. But this Article shall not apply to any person holding the office of president when this Article was proposed by the Congress, and shall not prevent any person who may be holding the office of President, or acting as President, during the term within which this Article becomes operative from holding the office of President or acting as President during the remainder of such term.